Gifted

A Guide for Mediums, Psychics, and Intuitives

Lisa Andres

D1018066

Cover Design by Regina Wamba
www.maeidesign.com

Editing by Patrick and April Durham
http://editingandebooks.com

ISBN:9781508745327

Library of Congress Control Number: 2015902310

CONTENTS

INTRODUCTION

This book is intended to be everything that I was looking for when I was just opening up and used books as my primary source of nourishment in developing, or trying to develop, my psychic and medium skills. I found lots of autobiographical stories, but there were not many books that would attempt to teach me *HOW* to do this kind of stuff. At the time, I really didn't even know what I was trying to do and was frustrated in not knowing how to open up.

In addition to opening to your psychic, medium and intuitive gifts, I have also included many other subjects to assist you on your journey. I added information about such things as Akashic records and past lives since you may have questions about those subjects. I also asked my students and peers what they would like to see in the book, which is how the chapter on spirit guides was born.

I knew I had been a medium my whole life. I had heard and seen *dead people* since I was a small child. On the television, there was a show called *Medium*. In advertisements for the show, there were commercials where the main character had a gang of dead people standing at the foot of her bed. I remember thinking, "That's ME!" I felt an immediate sense of relief knowing that I wasn't alone; there must be others out there like me.

I used to think I was constantly being chased by dead people and that being a medium was a curse. It scared me, too. Now I provide readings for others that are grieving the loss of their loved ones and know that it's not a curse; it's a gift to be able to do this work.

When I attended my first psychic development class in 2007, there was a plethora of information coming at me about many things concerning the paranormal. Some of it I found interesting, and there was a time or two I found myself not believing a thing I'd heard. I say that because you may likely read this book and have some very similar thoughts. That is okay. You will hear it when you are ready to hear it, and if you disagree with something I say, it's okay. What I am writing is my truth, and what I believe. It may or may not be yours.

The material in this book is non-denominational. I was raised in the Roman Catholic Church. I have since come to terms with the fact that not all things in this book are taught in the church, and likely in other denominations of Christianity or many other religions. I'm okay with that. I know that this is a gift from God and know that it is what I came to Earth to do. If you have fear with this material in regards to religion, it is likely a past life memory, and you can read more about that in this book. I will make reference to God and the universe often, and to me they are many times one in the same. If you are uncomfortable with either of those terms, please replace it with a term that encompasses the higher power, or all, to you.

Either way, if you are reading this book you are gifted. And your intuition is telling you that you *are* a psychic or intuitive, or you *are* a medium, or both. We are all here to help others heal through our work. I believe it's our contract on Earth, and that it's not a gift that God intended for us to keep for ourselves.

CHAPTER 1

MY STORY

My family moved from Buffalo, New York, to Minneapolis, Minnesota, when my mother was six months pregnant with me. Although I have never lived in New York, that move somehow shaped me more than my family knows. I was born on Father's Day, June 18, 1972. It was two weeks before my due date, but I am convinced I heard my father tell my mother the day before that he wanted me as a gift for Father's Day. To this day, my dad and I call it our special day. My parents were divorced before I could remember, and I grew up with my dad. Later, some extended family from the east coast joined us. Both parents remarried, but I never had siblings.

I started to see and sense spirits when I was a toddler. When I learned how to form what I saw into words, it was not well accepted by my Roman Catholic family. I got sent to a psychiatrist at around age seven, and I quickly learned what to say to make them believe I was over it. Early childhood was lonely for me. It was hard not to have brothers and sisters to play with and to be from another state. I did not care where I was born. I talked like them

1

and was their little New York clone. It was just enough to isolate me. I always knew I was different and longed to be normal. The first time I was bullied was on the bus on the way to kindergarten. I so desperately wanted to make friends with the other girls. One day, when I was tapped on the shoulder by two girls my age sitting behind me, I was relieved that they wanted to befriend me. Then, they sprayed perfume in my eye.

We moved out of the city and into a trailer park in the country when I was in grade school. The kids there were different, but they bullied me anyway. Every day, I used to walk to the bus stop and get beat up. I did not know what I was doing wrong, and I dreaded going to school. My dad worked the overnight shift then. He needed to find a babysitter that would take me overnight, and only one family would do that. When he drove me by their place to show me where I would be going, I screamed and cried. It was the home of the girl that bullied me the worst. He cried and apologized, but since we did not have much of a support group in Minnesota, I went to that babysitter anyway. They had a younger daughter my age that took me under her wing and taught me how to fight. In that place, it is what you had to do to survive going to school every day. I still know that friend to this day and will always be thankful I met her.

We moved, again, to a house nearer the city when I was in junior high school. I was not as afraid of bullies by then, but I was exhausted from a childhood of fighting to make my way. The bullies at the new school could sense me, though, and soon I was challenged. I was tired of fighting. I feel that my ability to see spirits must have gone dormant in those years. Or, perhaps, I just wasn't in touch with that ability because I did not have much peace while I was growing up.

When I was about 17, I started to sense the paranormal again. By age 20, all of the things I had suppressed or ignored for so long engulfed me. So many things were happening at once, I could not make heads or tails of it, but I knew it was paranormal. I could hear voices sometimes in the form of what seemed like chatter in my ear. I could see things moving sometimes; not only spirits, but actual physical objects. One night I saw my lip balm being carried across my room by some invisible force. I even felt spirits get into bed with me at night, which nearly unhinged me.

The one constant I had in the years that I started to open up again was my Grandma Ali. I could call her anytime day or night and tell her about the crazy things that happened to me, and she would listen and try to help me understand. I found out my mom had this ability, too. My mom and I lived together for the first time I could remember when I was about 20. We lived in what my mother refers to as *The House From Hell*. It was on Lake Minnetonka, a big lake near Minneapolis. In addition, there had been rumors of it having been built on some sort of sacred burial ground. That was enough to incite fear in both of us. One day, while I lived there, my mom and I thought we heard a noise in a vacant room in the home and went to explore it. When we both got in the room, we both saw the same ghost: a little girl holding a balloon in her hand. I remember we nearly trampled each other trying to both get out of the doorway at the same time because it scared us so much.

As my twenties progressed, the ability I had to see and sense spirits grew. I did not know what to do with it, and it mostly annoyed me. I learned to create boundaries with the spirit world, and, at first, that meant that they were only allowed to try to get my attention during my human daytime hours. They were very good at trying to get to me at night because I now realize I have my guard down more at night. I even had one ghost who would whistle to try to get my attention. I was always impressed by the lengths they would go to try to get my attention in those days.

After a divorce in my early thirties, I bought my first house alone. There was a housing boom at the time, and that meant I had to buy in the city. The house I bought was 100 years old, and, after an exhausting search, I knew it was mine from the moment I entered. Shortly after I moved in, two different people sitting in my living room said, "Do you know, I think I just saw a ghost in the other room?"

I had suspected as much, but that was affirmation. Over the few years I lived there, many more people told me there was a lot of spirit activity there.

During that time, I complained a lot to my Grandma Ali about how the spirits drove me nuts all the time. She would patiently tell me, again and again, that I was a medium and meant to help people. In those days, I was fighting it, and poor Grandma got the brunt of the fight. I used to scream that it was a curse and could not understand how I was meant to help people. Two other psychics also told me I was a medium during that time, but I still was not listening.

I finally opened my ears to what my Grandma was saying after a while. I decided to go to a beginning psychic development class nearby. It was taught by Echo Bodine, a well-known psychic medium that lives in Minneapolis. I did not see too much about actual medium training in the lesson plan, but I went anyway. I needed to open up all the things I had worked so hard to block in my youth and figured that was a start.

I remember the night before the class started. At the time, I was dating someone who I did not know how I was going to tell that I was going to a psychic class. The night before the first class, he dumped me. I was heartbroken, again, and not happy about it. I was screaming at the universe that it was not fair. I threatened not to go to class and not to use any of my psychic gifts. That very night was the first night I clearly heard my spirit guides. I heard, "That's fine, Lisa. You don't have to do this. But, if you don't do this, you may not stay on Earth much longer because it's part of your soul contract."

I had no idea what that all meant but knew I did not want to die. Deciding to err on the side of caution, I was at the first class the following day. After the 12-week class was over, I still wanted to know more about how to develop my skills as a medium. The Twin Cities that I live(d) in had so many psychics and mediums, but not one seemed to me that they were teaching what I was looking for. I finally made a plea to the universe one starry night that winter and threw my hands up asking for a medium teacher. I felt so desperate that in exchange for my plea, I offered to teach other mediums if needed. At the time, the thought of teaching mediums terrified me.

That Christmas, I received the book *Angels 101* by Doreen Virtue. I was mad. I had no idea who that was, and I did not want a book about angels! I remember I even asked my Grandma Ali (who gave it to me) for the receipt so I could exchange it. Suffice to say, the exchange never occurred. A few months later, I was in Hawaii going to medium training and certification with Doreen Virtue. At the time, I had no idea how I was going to get there. Once I applied and was accepted, all that I needed appeared. That weekend changed my life. She trained us to do readings for others and to do them on a platform for others. Platform readings are similar to what you might see on TV sometimes when mediums call dead people at random for strangers out of an audience. It was scary and wonderful at the same time. I passed all the required elements of a medium reading and was certified at the end of the series.

It was in Hawaii for medium training that Doreen Virtue's assistant suggested I should come back for Angel Therapy® training a couple of months later. It seemed like a neat idea, but I did not know how I had pulled off paying for one trip to Hawaii, let alone two. Well, you guessed it. Two months later, I was in Hawaii again, this time for the weeklong *Angel Camp*, as it is sometimes referred to, to be certified as an Angel Therapy Practitioner®.

When I returned to Minnesota after all of my training in Hawaii, I was troubled by the thought of my training being shelved and never trying readings for others because I was afraid. When my friend and teacher Echo was having a mini-expo, I asked her if she would let me have space to try to do readings for free for others so I could try it. She did, and she even put it in the email to her list of approximately 6,000 people. I did not have time to be nervous that first day. I had clients continually the whole day, which was about eight hours. I remember thinking I would only be doing medium readings for lost loved ones, and I was wrong. It was that day that I truly learned that mediums are also psychics. My first clients asked me about a lost item. I later learned that so many people wanted to see me that some had to be turned away. After that first event, Echo advised me to consider charging for my readings, and after that day I faced my fears and jumped in. A month or two after that, I started being asked by some of my peers to teach a medium class. It took ten or fifteen of them asking for me to realize I was being called to task by the universe for the promise I had made to teach others. Shortly thereafter, my medium classes were born. It has since evolved into other classes for psychics and intuitives, as well.

A breakup in 2009 caused me to reevaluate my life and realize I had always wanted to move to the east coast. I grew up with a family that was always telling me it was better out there. I had fallen in love with Boston the first time I had visited it years earlier and had been since warning my family of my desire to live there. In early 2010, I realized my dream and moved to the city I had always loved, Boston. It was scary to leave my home but liberating at the same time. My whole family had done the same thing years earlier, so at least I had them for support in hearing the stories of how they adjusted.

About a month into my move, the grief of feeling homesick hit. I cried like a machine, on and off, those first few months, and I came home to visit sooner than I had thought. And often. I had left a job of twelve years in Minneapolis, and I joined the same company when I moved to Boston. In my new office, the position did not fit me well. So, I changed my career a few months into my move. I remember thinking that I did not move out there to be miserable in my job. I went with a goal to stay for three years, and I ended up staying just over a year. The universe had other plans for me. My career had never really taken off out there, and the cost of living was too much to bear without a constant source of income as I had when I moved there.

In addition, my stepfather died somewhat suddenly from liver cancer at the age of 58. My mom was filled with grief. I had a knowing that I had to at least go home for a couple of months to be with her. I gave up my apartment and downsized the belongings I had due to the cost of moving and put what I had left in storage in Massachusetts. I was convinced I would be back. For that first month back in

Minnesota in the spring of 2011, I could not figure out why my life seemed to be falling apart. I left Boston with barely enough money to get home, and I left all my current sources of income in Boston. I was frustrated and did not understand why I was living at home again at the age of 38.

It took me a while to get out of my funk. I offered myself up to the universe as a full time psychic medium if that was what I was supposed to be, but that did not take shape at that time. So, I asked the universe for another corporate job. It is what I had been good at for twelve years before. I missed the security a job like that provided. After six months being home in Minnesota feeling lost, I started a corporate job. Ironically, it is working to settle the accounts of dead people. How is that for affirmation that I am a medium? Within a couple of months, I had my things shipped back from Boston and even got the same condo back I had lived in before I had left because I know the owner. It felt like deja vu because I had to buy back a lot of the furniture I had left on the curb in Boston, but I was happy to be home. I started facilitating a psychic support group of sorts with a peer right around the time I started my new job, and I even taught a couple more classes about psychic and medium topics.

Still, I felt empty. I was confident enough to be alone and do things alone. I have always been an extrovert, so I had to get out of the house sometimes because I recharge socially. If that meant going to see live music and doing other activities alone, that was how it had to be. My life did not turn out the way I had planned. I had wanted kids and a family which never materialized. I was still alone and more confused than ever. One night in July of 2012, I had a dream. Or, what I thought was a dream at the time. I died. Yes, died. In the dream, I remember waking up in my bed and seeing the golden light that seemed like it led to Heaven. I felt such peace. It surpassed any peace I had ever experienced as a human. So, I left my body and started to follow the light. I must have realized that I was going to leave Earth. All of the sudden, the thought of those I would hurt if I left was excruciating. I paused and said to whoever was listening, "Uh, you guys? I don't think I'm ready to leave Earth yet."

To which I heard, "Well, then WRITE THE BOOK!"

Wow. I had been told to write a book a few times before during readings provided to me by two other psychics and others who saw a story I wrote on Facebook about my move to and from Boston. Three different people who read that short story told me I should write a book. I always had a nagging feeling I should write a book, but it seemed a daunting task, so I never really did it. That dream scared me into action, and here I am. By the time this book is published, it will be about a year after that prophetic dream. I now realize how much I love writing and look forward to writing more.

My work as a psychic medium continues. I do readings for others and have plans to do my first solo medium gallery, which is a when I provide cold medium readings on stage for an audience to connect them with their deceased loved ones on the other side. I realize that part of my purpose is to help others with my gift, and I cannot believe how far I have come from the days that I thought it was a curse. A few days after the dream and heavenly command to write the book, I met my boyfriend. I was so cynical that I never thought love possible again, but I now realize I am not meant to be alone as I had feared. I sure am glad I decided to stay on Earth!

CHAPTER 2

LIGHTWORKERS AND LIFE PURPOSE

A lightworker is someone with a global purpose and an individual life purpose. A global purpose is a life purpose that helps others in some way, in addition to themselves. A lightworker may also be known as an Earth angel.

The generation known as Baby Boomers has many lightworkers among them. They came to Earth as the result of prayers for peace from Earth in the aftermath of World Wars I and II. The prayers brought an influx of babies who came to Earth to essentially help our planet.

The Earth continues to need help and prayers for peace. We are not the only planet in our solar system, and it is our job to keep peace on this planet and make positive changes. With the recent changes of energy that have brought many changes to our planet and our lives, perceived as both good and bad, we are needed more than ever to help conquer and usher out fear-based energy as well.

If you feel upset by a particular issue, this is a sign that it is likely part of your purpose to help in some way. It could be that pet abuse makes you mad because pets don't have a voice. It could be the potential change of a law, such as Gun Laws or GMO food labeling, which are hot topics right now in the USA. It could be anything. But when you continually hear information on the news and think to yourself, "Someone should DO something about that," that someone is you.

Lightworkers are here to help others. It could be through work in their community. It could be to become a lawyer, police officer or other civil servant that helps with justice in some way. It could be whatever we are called to do that impacts others in addition to ourselves.

The bottom line is that a lightworker brings positivity to more than just themselves. This is not a particularly easy time on Earth right now. If you have felt that this is not an easy time, there are others out there who have felt it perhaps even more intensely than you. We have come to a point where our presence on Earth is a powerful, positive thing, and we inhabit bodies for a reason. That is so we will no longer be invisible and will have a presence to be able to take action we are need for at this time. No one said it would be easy, but our souls agreed to be here at this time of need. It will be worth helping others in the ways that we feel called. For many of us, that is the only way we feel fulfilled.

Many of us experience delay tactics to our soul's purpose. That could be something such as drinking too much, eating too much, complaining too much, or thinking, "I'm not good enough or strong enough." Delay tactics can be anything preventing you from doing what feels good to you. If you are drinking to try to quell your frustration, it is likely a delay tactic. If reading this passage just made you mad, you likely have been doing that very thing: delaying your soul's true mission on Earth. It is okay, the time is now, and your intention of learning more about your true mission is your soul's way of waking up. You are loved and supported by the universe in whatever choice you make, especially on your true mission to help others on Earth.

For some of us, the way that we help others is as simple as kindness to others. There are many of us out there that feel like we want to just blend into the background. We may be very good at something such as computers or technology. Or we may just be a cashier at the local market. But in doing the very duties that others may consider mundane, we lightworkers are achieving our life purpose by being kind to others and helping others. This kindness and love creates an atmosphere of peace, which is needed on Earth. It is collectively so powerful that it keeps our planet intact and safe from any destruction such as nuclear war. We are not the only planet in our solar system, and there is a universal benefit to the Earth staying a part of the solar system, for it would disrupt planetary alignment if we did not exist.

I remember when my day job had a fundraiser where you could give out Valentine's greetings with a candy bar on Valentine's Day. I bought thirty or so, thinking I would send them to all my business partners and friends just to do something nice. When I came into work the day they were given out, I had forgotten all about it. When I got to the floor, many had already received them, and there was an air of joy on the floor. I suddenly had an understanding of how just one kind act can improve the collective energy of consciousness.

If you are reading this and think to yourself, "I don't know what my purpose is as a lightworker," that's okay. You do not have to know exactly what it is today. If you have felt a sense of frustration in knowing you have a purpose and just can't figure out what it is, that is a sign that you are indeed a lightworker and have a global mission to help others in addition to a personal mission.

What is your passion? Have you always wanted to sing or entertain others? Have you wanted to start your own business? Have you had an idea of what you would like to do but have no idea how to do it? Well, that's likely a calling card from the universe saying it's time to wake up.

I believe that anyone trying to help others is a lightworker that has a life purpose of helping others. You likely have other things you are doing. I'm a musician. I'm an author. I'm a medium. We lightworkers can be dynamic multitaskers who are good at many things.

That frustration and/or anxiety you are feeling is your soul's way of saying there is something you should be doing. Your feelings are the compass pointing you in the direction you are meant to go. You may not know the answers today, and that is okay. Just go in the direction that feels good and know that you will get there one step at a time. A life purpose unfolds as you take the journey that is life. It is often said that those that have overcome and suffered the most have the biggest life purpose.

I had gotten to the point where I could not figure out why activities that used to bring me joy or make me content, such as watching TV all night on the couch after a long day of work, were now causing me discontent and frustration. I could not, for the life of me, figure out why I felt so frustrated. So, at first, I would try to drink it away with beer. The next day, the same frustration would appear, and the cycle would start again. I felt that I had been guided for many years to write a book. It was not until I finally sat down to write this book that the sense of frustration went away and was replaced by peace. I still fight this feeling daily and likely will until the book is finished.

I cannot tell you that I have honestly figured out all of my life purpose. There are things that I feel are on my bucket list, so to speak, that may hold a key to shaping my life purpose. I have always wanted to write a book. I have always wanted to be a mother. I have always wanted to repair a home in neglect. I tried to push the house repair (i.e., "I want to flip houses") as not being part of my purpose, and then I realized how it all works together. There are many houses that need the love and restoration that I may be able to provide. Even if it's one house at a time, that has the potential to heal and restore energy. As I said earlier, it all works on a collective consciousness to restore peace. A love of homes and real estate is one of the lights in my soul that has just never stopped shining. I may have put it on the backburner for a few years, but it always comes to the surface.

If you are an intuitive, a psychic, or a medium, then you have likely found a part of your life purpose. But that may not be all there is to it. You probably have different roles, such as a parent, a teacher, or whatever else it is you are doing at this very moment. Life happens one day at a time. Do what makes you happy. Stop the things that make you unhappy. Even if that one thing that you have been dreaming of seems unattainable, start to believe it's possible and take the steps to lead you toward that. It does not have to happen all at once. If you worry about making the wrong choice, know this: your path follows you. There are no mistakes, only lessons and growth.

When I was a child, I thought I knew what my life purpose was: to sing. I cracked from the womb singing to the top of my lungs and was convinced that I was going to be a famous rock star someday. This evolved into an early lifetime of preparation, which eventually led me to graduate from a college of music. I spent many years in cover bands and dreamed of writing my own music and having a record deal someday. I was completely aghast when I received a psychic reading where I was told music was just a hobby for me. My true occupation was in psychic and medium work.

I now realize that music may not have been my primary purpose in life, but it helped to shape me into who I am today, and there's purpose in that. Since a piece of my path involves public speaking, being onstage and speaking to an audience in between songs prepared me for this.

How many times have you perhaps thought, "I wouldn't change my past, for it made me who I am today"? You never know where the future may lead you. Try to find peace with the current moment and believe in your dreams. Your main life purpose has already been accomplished, for you are here on Earth. You are so important to this Earth right now. You are loved and supported by the heavens, even though sometimes it feels that you are alone. There are always angels, your spiritual team, and deceased loved ones around you. They are rooting for you, are proud of you, and love you for exactly who you are.

NOTES

CHAPTER 3

LIFE PURPOSE AURAS

Life Purpose Auras are different than what you would normally associate with an aura photo, the kind where you see your figure surrounded by red, green, or yellow energy. A Life Purpose Aura is closer to you or your client, similar to an eggshell or the hard coating on a piece of candy such as a jaw breaker. It's the thin layer right around your skin and in between that larger aura that you sometimes see in aura photos. You will have many clients that will ask you what their life purpose is. One of the best ways to tune into that is to tune in to their Life Purpose Aura.

The best way to see your client's Life Purpose Aura is intuitively, such as when you are doing a psychic or intuitive reading for a client. Take a moment and close your eyes and imagine your client. What color do you see that seems to represent an outline around his or her shape? That's the Life Purpose Aura.

Below are the colors of the Life Purpose Auras and what they mean in regards to your clients and their life purpose. It is entirely possible that your clients may have two colors, which means they have more than one life purpose, of course. Use your intuitive senses when relaying this to a client, and as with the intuitive readings, it's best to first try this out on people you know. Hopefully this information can help you if you are already in, or planning on going into, a practice reading for clients in some way.

Life Purpose Aura Colors

Blue: This is a medium-blue color. It means communicator and/or artist. This is a person that likely has some sort of artistic talent and also has a life purpose to communicate to others. It may be to communicate his or her art (such as musician), or it could be to become a public speaker. People with this Life Purpose Aura may be called to be writers of a book or a blog.

Green: This is the Life Purpose Aura of a healer. It could represent either a traditional doctor or health professional, or a non-traditional healer of some sort, such as Reiki master, Qi Gong practitioner, and more. It could also include those that work to heal pets in some way. It may also indicate that your client has the ability to heal others by listening to them or giving advice.

Yellow: This can either be an eggshell color or bright yellow. This person is a perpetuator of peace. Think of some that have been associated with peace such as the Dalai Lama or Mother Theresa. If your client has this Life Purpose Aura, he or she may be involved in a traditional means of bringing peace such as the Peace Corps, philanthropy, or volunteer work of some kind.

Dark Blue: This person is an Indigo: here to speak truth, find truth, and help to bring changes that are positive in a strong but peaceful way. They likely have a *warrior* type of energy, and they may feel guided to make some substantial life changes associated with their life purpose and the changes that they would like to see.

Rainbow: This Life Purpose Aura literally looks like it is multicolored, similar to a rainbow. If you see this on your client, this is a *star* person who has a connection to other planets. They may be a Reiki Master, have a fascination with UFO's, and/or work with computers in some way. They may also like dolphins.

Bright Purple: This is a Life Purpose Aura associated with religion or spirituality. This is a person who wants to serve others through being involved religiously, such as an ordained minister or working with the church. They may also be someone on a very spiritual path, although it may not be with a traditional church.

Eggplant Purple (a darker purple): This is the Life Purpose Aura associated with a medium or hospice worker. This person is someone who works either with the dead after they have crossed over or works with those still alive to help them transition to the other side.

Aqua Green/Blue: This is a teacher and healer combination. This person is likely a spiritual teacher. Perhaps this person is meant to teach others healing. They may also be an entrepreneur that teaches others and heals others in some way as well. This is an example of a dual life purpose where you may see these two colors together, such as blue on top of green.

LISA ANDRES

NOTES

CHAPTER 4

THE LAW OF ATTRACTION

As a psychic, medium or intuitive, you have an important life purpose. That life purpose likely involves service to others with your gift. That is where the *law of attraction* comes in to play. The principle of the law of attraction is that like attracts like. Basically, you receive whatever it is that occupies your thoughts. So, if you think about how bad your life is all the time and wonder why it is not getting better, it is probably because you are obsessing about what you DO NOT want. The universe does not differentiate emotion. Alignment of the law of attraction just hears, "My life is bad." Then, the universe orders it up for you. Suffice to say, try to keep your thoughts positive and think about only that which you desire. If you have done more negative thinking than positive lately, this change does not have to be done overnight. A little at a time. Try to correct your negative thoughts by saying the same thing in a more positive way. Instead of "I hate my job," think "I have a job that I love."

When you make a wish, you send a rocket of desire out into the universe. When you send that rocket of desire out into the universe, let it go and *trust* that it will manifest. Worrying about it, in essence, is like preventing that rocket from getting to its intended target. So, think about only what you desire. The thoughts of a lightworker are very powerful and have the capacity to manifest quickly. Would it not be much better to manifest your dreams rather than your worries? The universe also loves and responds consistently to gratitude. So, even if this very moment is one that does not feel good to you, what is it that you can find to be grateful about?

When I snuggle into my bed at night, I sometimes think to myself "I love my bed" or "I love this apartment that I live in." It can be something simple for which to be grateful. If you just had some sort of fender bender in your car, try to be grateful that it was not worse. If you are frustrated with your financial situation, try to bless and love the one you have now. Bless and be grateful for the money you have now and the bills that you are able to pay now.

In a way similar to the law of attraction, positive affirmations are a way of confirming our desires to both us and the universe. "I am a bestselling author." "Today is a going to be a great day." "I attract kindness everywhere I go." "I'm worthy of great love." "I attract a wonderful, new, romance into my life." Even if you have a hard time believing it as you say it, fake it until you make it. Every day you will feel a little better as you say each affirmation.

One that I have been saying lately is: "I have a career that I love, working for and with people I love that love me. I make more money than I could imagine." I said affirmations to attract my soul mate for four months before he arrived. I felt like everything was right in my life, but the one thing that consistently never worked out for me was love relationships. And, in believing that, it had become part of my vibration. The romantic relationships I had been attracting never worked out because my vibration and thought patterns said so.

At first, I started saying these affirmations afraid that I might actually receive the man of my dreams. I had been a natural cynic up until that point. I also said them still believing in my conscious mind that romance never worked out for me. Still I persisted, and the affirmations eventually changed my vibration and allowed me to attract what I wanted into my life. I now have the romance I had dreamed of, with the kind of guy I did not think existed for me, because I believed in the affirmations. So, do not be surprised if what you affirm appears.

You might be wondering, "Why is this in a book on how to be a medium, psychic, or intuitive?" You need to feel secure in your life before your energy is most available to help others, and the angels want you to have all of your physical and emotional needs met so you can focus on your true purpose of helping others. You can start to create that which you desire with positive affirmations and the law of attraction.

NOTES

CHAPTER 5

PROTECTION AND CLEARING

Protection

It's a good practice to always ask for protection from God, spirit, or the source that you believe in or feel guided to. I most commonly call on Archangel Michael and the goddess Isis for protection. I ask Archangel Michael to guard and protect me in all that I do. I may ask angels to go to the four corners of my house and protect it and keep it safe and to also do that with my car, my work, and the same for all of my loved ones.

Free will is a factor when trying to send protection to others, so you may want to say, "I want to send this person angels for whatever it is he needs," or "I want angels to protect my friend, with his soul's permission." The client may not consciously know or be ready to hear it, and you then are doing this with integrity by knowing you are not doing anything without permission.

Clearing

My favorite way of clearing is the kind that doesn't require any human tools. It is by intention and asking for help from the angels. I usually ask Archangel Michael to come in and to clear the energy in a room; I ask him to cut the energetic cords of fear in the room and to vacuum the room and fill it with light. In addition, there are things that you can use to clear a space of negative energy such as sage, palo santo wood, Florida water, or candles.

You can usually find sage loose or in a stick. You usually want to light it and then blow it out, leaving the smoke to go to the areas where you want to clear the energy. You may also use a fan of some sort (many use feather fans) to help circulate the smoke. It will naturally cleanse the negative energy.

Palo santo wood works in the same way. It just smells a bit sweeter and is sometimes called sweet palo santo wood. It has been used since ancient times, originating in Peru, to cleanse negative energy.

Florida water is a citrusy type of cologne water, and some believe its use stemmed from the fountain of youth. I pour some in a spray bottle and dilute it with water. You can use it as it is or dilute it as much or as little as you want. It has a very high vibration, so even watered down it's still very effective at cleansing negative energy. I use it as I feel guided, as should you. It comes in handy in an instance where it's not appropriate to have the smoke of sage or palo santo. I most commonly use it in instances where I am in someone's home doing a clearing or reading.

Candles can be used in cooperation with any of these tools to increase energy in a room. Get any scent you feel guided to, or connect with, because it is likely that your energy works in cooperation with that scent. I find it particularly helpful to have at least one candle lit when I am doing a reading for a client.

You can use any of these tools, and if you don't know where to start, seek them out at a local store or on the Internet and see which one you feel most guided to. There is not a right or wrong: it's what you feel is right for you and your personal space or practice.

Mirrors

Mirrors have an energy that can act in one of two ways. It can attract negative energy, or it can deflect it. For instance, I usually don't keep mirrors in my bedroom because I believe that they can channel and keep negative energy in the room.

I do, however, use mirrors as a means of protection, if you will. When I lived in an apartment, I put a pocket-sized mirror facing down in the bedroom under my bed to deflect any negative energy that might come from the apartment below me.

I also carry a pocket-size mirror facing the outside of my purse (inside my handbag) to deflect the negative energy that might happen from being in crowds and being around other people. I have even seen necklaces with small mirrors facing out as a means of protection that you can wear on your person.

Crystals

In my first psychic development class, I remember everyone there was talking about crystals. They carried them with them in their pockets or handbags, kept them in between their mattresses, you name it. Even when I helped my grandma move, she had a heavy box of what she called her "good crystals." I remember thinking, "Huh? They're rocks."

The first time I received a healing with a crystal, or rock as you might call it, I was in Hawaii. There was a spiritual shop there with crystals, and when I walked in, the woman offered me a healing with an angelite crystal. I didn't know what that was, but it sure felt like it cleared me.

That opened me up to the healing power of crystals. I would go to shops that had crystals and just grab the ones I felt guided to; I didn't need to know why. Then I bought a book to tell me what some of the crystals were and about their healing properties.

I started to keep some crystals that would help me deflect negative energy. Now I have become one of those people that carry rocks in my handbag and have them in my home, too. I have some that I have no idea why I have them, but I know that it feels better for me to have them. I love agates; I always have one on me and hold one to ground me when I am giving a reading.

You may want to look into something like *The Crystal Bible* by Judy Hall as a resource to use crystals as a means of protection, for clearing, or more.

NOTES

CHAPTER 6

THE SELF-CARE OF A MEDIUM, PSYCHIC OR INTUITIVE

It is important that you, as mediums, psychics, and intuitives, take care of yourselves because your body is the vessel that delivers messages to the people you help. Some do tend to use food, drink, or other chemicals to dull the heavy empathic emotions that we feel. We just have to remember moderation. It's never a good idea to give readings for others when you have had any sort of alcohol or drugs, as this attracts lower energies. You want to be sober when you deliver readings because you want the highest possible energy present.

Your body is a conduit for information. When I started doing readings, I wish that someone would have told me how tiresome it can be. Whether you are doing one reading or several, being a conduit for information is exhausting.

Sometimes I do all-day events where I provide readings for eight hours at a time. On the evening before, I make sure that I rest and try to get a good night's sleep. I also make sure that I have plenty of water near me throughout the day of the event, and I take breaks to both eat and ground myself. The first time I did an event like that I had no idea how exhausting it would be. I didn't break for food or anything. When it was over, I was so exhausted that I nearly had to be carried out of there. Now I make sure to always take breaks and eat during the day of an event. It helps me provide better readings to those that need my assistance.

NOTES

CHAPTER 7

BOUNDARIES

When you are doing readings or psychic work in general, you want to use good boundaries. This means that you don't give anyone a reading without their permission. If I intuit something about a person that I'm with, I don't just blab it out. If I feel strongly guided, I may ask them if they WANT the reading or information that I am receiving, and asking would be a good boundary. Just blurting it out to a stranger would not.

I can almost hear the question about television shows you may have seen where a psychic or medium walks up to a stranger and just reads them at random. I guess that makes good TV, but I still think it lacks boundaries. I am not judging that: I just don't encourage you to do anything like that if you can avoid it. At the very least, if you are feeling strongly guided to give a stranger a reading, ask permission first.

When you are giving a reading, a good boundary is to not give a third-party reading. A third-party reading is when someone asks about the sister of a friend, their boyfriend's thoughts, etc. Make sure that you have the permission of the person who is being asked about. If a client asks about a person such as his or her sister or son, use your intuition as to how to answer.

You have three choices:

1. Ask if the client has the person's permission.

2. Disclose that you don't do third-party readings.

3. Close your eyes and tune into the soul of this person to ask or ascertain his or her permission.

When a client gives you permission for a reading, and once you start the reading, remember that any information you are receiving is intended for your client. Whether you like what you are hearing or not, remember, nothing would come to you that the client wouldn't want or say. Then you know that you are safe, and the information you are receiving is for the client's greatest and highest good.

NOTES

CHAPTER 8

BLOCKS

Your ego is the biggest block you have in being able to listen to and trust your intuition in doing readings or even knowing and familiarizing yourself on a conscious level with your spiritual team. That would be the voice that's telling you that you're not good enough or not wise enough to do this work. The one that says, "Oh, that person is such a better psychic or medium than I am," or, "Who am I to be doing this?"

The most common block that people tell me they have is a block from past lives. An example would be, "I feel that I have abused my psychic gifts in another life, and now they are blocked in this life." I think people say or think this for one of two reasons. The first is that it's true, and it very well may be. If that's the case, it's always possible to get a past life healing from a qualified practitioner or healer. The second is that it's your ego telling you that you are not good enough to do this. That is a very natural procrastination tactic of your soul's purpose. Many of us have past life fears of coming out of the spiritual closet for this work. And a block, whether real or perceived, is one.

Even if it is truly a block, it can be healed.

When I refer to "ego", it is as opposed to our "soul." I believe that when we feel bad, it's our body's opposition with our soul. Our soul knows our true purpose is to be doing this work. It's our ego that's telling us no.

I think back to when I first started doing readings. I was so frustrated with feeling blocked because all of the bad experiences of my childhood were shutting them down. I had no idea how to do a reading then, and the thought of teaching and writing a book about this would have severely scared me.

Anything is possible. Trust that you will know all the answers and move past the blocks at the exact right time and order sequence. The best thing that happened to me was finding a teacher who saw similar things and provided me with some tools to affirm that I was seeing it correctly. You will, too, if that is what you want. It is often said that when the student is ready, the teacher appears.

NOTES

CHAPTER 9

BAD SPIRITS

I am often asked if there are bad spirits or evil spirits. Evil is not a word I believe in. I do not claim to be an authority on the idea that evil does or does not exist. But I believe that if evil exists, humans created it.

Every scary spirit I have ever encountered was just a spirit in need of healing. I have never had one try to harm me because I'm there to help them.

When I lived in Boston, I saw one spirit in my own home that I thought was a vampire. It momentarily scared me, and I'm not easily scared by these kinds of spirits anymore. I realized that it was a person who, in real life, was into vampires. That persona followed them to the other side. I helped this spirit heal and saw a beautiful soul come out of it and go to the light.

Have you ever seen paranormal shows where the ghost hunter becomes scratched from a spirit? I do not believe that it's not possible. I just don't have any technical experience *ghost hunting*. I believe that if it happens, it's simply the "you kick a dog, he'll bite you" principle. I don't go to upset the spirits and have not been harmed in the line of business, so to speak. I ask the angels for protection and trust that I'm protected.

NOTES

CHAPTER 10

THE CLAIRS

You perhaps have heard of clairvoyance. The terms I will describe, in brief, are the different types of clairs (from the French *clair*, meaning "clear"):

- **Clairvoyance:** The ability to SEE psychic information

- **Clairaudience:** The ability to HEAR psychic information

- **Clairsentience:** The ability to FEEL (touch) psychic information

- **Claircognizance:** The ability to KNOW psychic information (You don't know how you know; you just know it.)

- **Clairalience:** The ability to SMELL psychic information

- **Clairgustance:** The ability to obtain psychic information through TASTE

There may be other clairs, but these are the ones I resonate with the most. You may have some of them, or you may have all of them. You may not know if you have any at all. That's okay.

Chances are good that you have more than one of these. I resonate with each of them in some way or the other. The only one I don't recall ever having or using is clairgustance. The one that I resonate with the most is claircognizance. That is: I don't know how I know; I just know it. You may be different and identify with one now, and then find that as you develop your skill set, you find you possess and use many different clairs.

In my early years, I remember a clear sense of clairalience. Every woman in my mother's family has an extraordinary sense of smell; meaning that I have felt at times that my nose rivals a canine's. I have heard many times that psychics have heightened senses, but let's just say that early in life I learned how to hold my nose without touching it and had times I wished I could turn off my extraordinary olfactory perception. Later I learned that this could help me identify departed loved ones. Every time my deceased great grandmother was near, I could smell the soap she used that I associated with her. As time went by, I developed clairaudience. When dead people were near, I could hear voices, coughing, or even whistling.

I'm primarily left-brained (logical and analytical), so it took a while before clairvoyance came into the picture. And when it did, I resisted. When I started to do readings, I had a very specific idea of how it was going to happen and told my guides the left-brained things I'd like to hear (spelled words, numbers, etc.). So what happened? My guides started to show me pictures, which just *hurt* to try to see at first! I realize, now, they did that just to help me develop my clairvoyance, and now it's second nature to me. When

I do readings now, there are many clairs that come into play. I can't say that I'm really thinking about which one it is or is not, I'm just grateful that I have the various clair tools in my chest, so to speak, to help me relay a message to a client.

Clairvoyance evolved into claircognizance. I didn't know where the information was coming from: it just came out in the message I was relaying. Here's a good example of claircognizance: you know how you sometimes get a phone call, and you just knew the person was going to call? That is claircognizance!

You do not have to remember all of these labels. They are just intended as a point of reference for you as you learn. The best way to get this in your own way is to have an idea of what clair you want, have, or don't have. It was not until I got out of my own way and stopped thinking that I had to see or hear things a certain way, that the information started coming to me more freely.

NOTES

CHAPTER 11

HOW DO I KNOW IF I'M A PSYCHIC OR AN INTUITIVE?

Do you relate to the word *empathy* or *empathic*? Have you always felt that you can absorb the emotions of others, for good or bad, and it's excruciating to sometimes be in strenuous emotional situations as a result? Does being empathic sometimes feel as if it drains your energy?

You often seem to notice that people have always been able to confide their deepest, darkest secrets to you. You don't know what it is about you and have thought it must just be a *vibe* you give off. You are likely in a profession known for listening to others problems, such as a therapist or even a bartender. Maybe you've even joked you should be one.

More than once you knew the answers ahead of time, like who was about to call when you picked up the phone. You've joked, or someone else has, that you *must be psychic*.

Sometimes you just seem to be on a roll guessing things of no consequence, such as a baby pool at work (when the baby would come, etc.), or who was going to make it to the basketball final four. You always just seem to know what song is going to play before it plays.

You probably have had a hint of intuition more than once that you didn't listen to. You may have thought to yourself more than once, "I should have listened to my hunch and taken a different road to work," when you are sitting there in traffic because a traffic accident has now caused an unexpected delay.

Have you always had the uncanny ability to read people or just been a really good judge of character? You don't know how you know; you can just know. You're always right, no matter how others may disagree with you or no matter how long that validation takes. Not that you really needed the validation. You knew you were right from the get-go.

Throughout life, you have likely been impatient with a traditional classroom setting. It was not because you didn't want to learn; you just always felt smarter than the teachers or knew what you needed to learn did not exist in that classroom setting.

You likely have a fear of coming out of the *psychic closet*. It's scary to think of what your family and friends might do if they knew. The thought of the Salem Witch Trials gives you the shivers. This is likely because your soul knows of a time when others (maybe even you) were persecuted for those gifts.

The good news is that now you live in a time where you are SAFE. You were born to do this. You came here to help others with the gift of your psychic, intuitive, or empathic senses.

If you have nodded your head in agreement at several of

the things I have mentioned, then you are, indeed, psychic, intuitive and/or empathic.

The Term Psychic Versus Intuitive

I am a psychic. I get defensive that someone might call me something that I'm not. So I never felt that I associated too much with the word intuitive.

One day, when I got off the phone with a client for whom I had just done a psychic reading, I realized that a lot of my readings seemed to contain life coaching of sorts. Just then a term popped into my head: *Intuitive Life Coach.* I had never thought that I would think of myself as such a thing, and that was a way for me to connect with a term I was not sure applied to me. So to me, the terms psychic and intuitive are sometimes interchangeable.

An intuitive connects most with claircognizance, or the "I don't know how I know; I just know it." They tend to intuit answers from within. Psychics may access many of the clairs and associate most with clairvoyance or something similar. They are usually channeling information directly from their guides or spiritual team.

An intuitive is a person who just knows and feels the answer which is right. They may just know the answer, or they listen to their intuition as to which way to guide their client. Either is correct, and both are guided in very similar ways. You can use the term that resonates with you the most. Or you can use them both. There's no wrong answer.

NOTES

CHAPTER 12

HOW TO DO A PSYCHIC
OR INTUITIVE READING

Oracle Cards

One of the best ways to start doing psychic readings is with the use of oracle cards. Pick a deck that you feel drawn to and don't worry about knowing or not knowing how to do the spreads. My favorite decks are by Doreen Virtue. I started with one deck, the *Healing with the Fairies Oracle Cards*, by Doreen Virtue, and now I have several different decks that I use. I also usually go to the deck to which I feel guided, both physical card decks and also smartphone app decks that are available to most smartphones. When I use oracle cards, I usually go with the number of cards I feel guided to draw, but if you are a person that likes to follow the rules, so to speak, there's usually a guidebook in the front that tells you a little bit about the meaning of the cards and their spreads.

When you first get your oracle card deck, make sure to clear it. The deck has been touched by others; those that made it, packaged it, and even shipped the cards. You want to first unwrap them. Then go through the deck card-by-card and simply make sure you touch each of the cards. This act infuses the cards with your energy. Silently ask the angels, or whomever you feel guided to, to clear the cards. There were many people that touched them when they were produced, so you want to clear that energy. I usually also use something to clear them with, such as sage or palo santo wood. To do this, lay the cards out on a surface near you, and lay them out face up. I do this in a sort of fanning motion, so I can see a portion or most of all the cards. Then shuffle them a few times, and you should be ready to use them.

First, try a reading for yourself. Either think of a question or intention (such as your love life, for instance) before shuffling, and then draw three cards that represent the past, present and future, left to right, which is a common spread for oracle cards. There's no way you can choose the wrong card because the cards vibrate to the law of attraction. It's one of my favorite things to do if I have questions about myself, since I can do readings for other people but am not as objective with myself.

If you feel like it, start practicing on friends or family. You can even continue to do readings just for yourself for a while. I'm always amazed at how I receive the same cards again and again until whatever it's about passes. It's affirmed further when I do a reading for a friend because then I will see cards that somehow I have never seen in my own readings that come up for the friend.

You may even feel connected to make oracle cards a part of your business when you do readings for clients. There are many lightworkers that do. When a client asks you a question, feel free to draw a card from your oracle card deck. Say your client asks you about their job, and you draw a card. You might draw something like *Break Free* which is a card featured in Doreen Virtue's *Healing with the Fairies Oracle Cards*. At first, when doing this for practice on yourself or your friends, close your eyes for a brief moment and see what it is that comes to you in relation to that card for that client. If you feel you need some clarity or further information, draw another card. A client usually doesn't want to hear you read the words from the book, but you can definitely use it as a guide.

When I was learning to use cards and practicing readings on others, I would first ask my client's question and then draw a card. I'd look at the card, as would the client, and then I would just say whatever came to me in relation to the card. If you feel like you need the assistance of the book for a while, or even as affirmation to what you've said, that's okay. You may eventually feel like you want to try to do readings without the oracle cards. Whether you are using oracle cards or not, first let's discuss the types of readings you'll usually see.

Types of Psychic Readings

The majority of clients consistently ask questions on one or many of the following categories:

- Career
- Health
- Relationships
- Life Purpose

You may be guided to one or more of those topics, but what's more likely is that your clients will guide you with their questions. For instance, I seem to mainly get questions about life purpose and career. Those are things that I most naturally relate to because I have personally given both plenty of thought.

I originally thought I was only a medium. WRONG. I found out later that all mediums are also psychic. It was my clients that taught me this. The first time I sat down to give readings, I thought everyone coming to me was going to ask about dead people. I quickly found out that was not the client's only agenda. Now, I provide as many psychic readings as I do medium readings. And guess what? They are usually about one of the four main subjects I've listed.

You may find out in the process of doing readings that there's one thing you get asked about the most or prefer over others. Say, for instance, it is love and romance. People love that stuff! I had a student in one of my classes, and that was all she did. She was so good at it, and she even did a cold reading for me. She was right! She told me I would meet someone, and she described the boyfriend that I met a few months later to a tee. Neither of us knew that at the time, of course. It was just something at which she was really good, and she truly seemed to enjoy telling people about romance in their life.

I also had another student who seemed frustrated with the process of using oracle cards. He just seemed to feel blocked when doing a reading with the cards. As we talked, he naturally started to read correctly the people in some of the situations I was speaking about. He'd say, "Does he have dark hair and a stern look on his face?", or "Does she have long blonde hair?" You get the idea. I said, "Wow, you're *good* at this!" We then talked about how that might help him focus on the kind of readings to provide for others.

As I have said, the majority of my psychic readings seem to be about life purpose and career. And those are things that I most naturally relate to because I have given both of those lots of energy and thought. Generally speaking, though, I don't limit myself to psychic specialty, but you may feel it is right for you to do so. You may or may not have a specialty. The odds are good that you will learn more about that sort of thing as you go along. All of your readings may take a theme. You may just find that you love one type of reading more than others. Maybe you're a life coach or a medical intuitive. If you feel drawn to be a medical intuitive of any kind, it's important that you disclose to your client that you are not a medical doctor (unless you are) and that they should always see a medical doctor or health practitioner for their concerns.

When a client books an appointment with me, I usually ask them to have a few questions or an intention (like career, life purpose, etc.). I feel that most clients have a question whether they think they do or not. I ask the client to have a question or intention because a specific question gets a faster answer. Say a client books a short reading, or they've never had a reading. In the latter instance, we're talking about someone whose guides haven't had a chance to be consciously heard in this lifetime, so they all try to speak at once—about everything. It makes it a bit more difficult to get straight to the point, and you want to help your client make the most of her time with you. When I confirm the appointment and details with my client, I then set an intention myself. I ask my spiritual team to talk to the spiritual team of my client and make sure that we get her the best information possible, in the greatest and highest good for both of us, in the reading.

Personally, I have also decided that I don't like giving bad news if I can avoid it. Have you ever had a reading from someone and walked away feeling worse than when you started? I like to provide my clients with an uplifting experience, and I put that intention out there for my readings. It's not only for the client's sake, but my own as well. If you're paying for a reading, you generally do it to feel better, right? When the occasional bad news comes up, I know that it's supposed to. It's also possible that the client doesn't think the message is bad news, anyway. The important thing to keep in mind is that you are the messenger. It is not about you. You are just the vessel that delivers the message. Whatever comes out during the reading is a part of the reading.

The Reading

I usually do not use divination tools of any type during my readings. Before each reading, I generally light some palo santo wood, which to me clears as well as sage and smells a bit better, and clear the space around me.

As I start the reading, I usually hold onto an agate. I love agates. They ground me. I learned this from seeing one of my peers hold a crystal during her readings, and for some reason I have always felt led to do that. It doesn't give me the answers, of course, and I don't have to have one to provide the reading. I believe that the agate just keeps me grounded during the process of the reading. When I hold the agate in my hand, it is also a way that I signal to the spirit that I am ready to begin. You may have a way that you do this, too, even if you do not consciously know it. For instance, you could rub your hands together at the beginning of the reading or clear your throat. Maybe you say a prayer as the reading begins. It puts forth the sacred energy and your intention to become the vessel delivering the message.

Then I usually talk to clients and ask if they have a question or intention for the reading. If I feel guided to, I may make a small introduction of how the reading works (which is the case sometimes if a client has never had a reading). Other than that, I go right into the reading. I know that some of my peers sometimes say a prayer to bring the greatest and highest good guides, teachers, etc. in to help. If you want to do that, please do.

When you start a reading, *anything* that happens during the reading is part of the reading. This means that the minute you sit down with or speak to a client and the client asks you a question, the reading begins. All of the thoughts in your head now pertain to your client. Anything you sense or that happens in any way during the space of that reading is part of the reading. Anything. Even a laugh you randomly hear from someone in the next room. If you start to perspire, it's part of the reading. If you think about the fight you had with your lover that morning, it is part of the reading. If you are frustrated because you don't know how to translate the message or aren't getting a message, that's part of the reading.

On days when I have an appointment booked for a reading with a client, and on a personal level I have had a bad day, it sometimes will be part of the reading for my client. I had a reading occur on a day that I was emotionally exhausted from stress. By the time I started the reading, I still felt stressed and felt guided to mention that in the reading. I said to the client, "I feel like you have been worrying a lot lately and are emotionally exhausted," which the client confirmed.

Sometimes I get readings from other psychics. During a recent reading I received, the psychic said to me, "I can't figure out if this is me, or the angels—it's hard for me to separate." Well, there truly is no separation. If you are thinking it, it's part of the reading and from the angels. If you think it's from the angels, *IT IS* from the angels.

During the reading, your spiritual team pulls things out of your head like it's a database that they are accessing a file from. Even if you have a thought you believe might be getting in the way of the reading, it usually means that it is something that your client needs to know. It's part of the reading. *Trust* that. There are no wrong answers you give because whatever messages you relay, you are supposed to relay. Truly. I have had times where I have thought to myself after a reading, "I should have said this; I should have said that." We all do. But I realized that anything we are supposed to say or convey during the reading comes out. If we didn't say it, we likely weren't supposed to. Maybe the client just wasn't ready to hear the information.

If you can find someone to practice with, even two people, you can all take turns trying readings for each other. Start with one person asking a question while the other(s) takes time to write whatever she feels for a few minutes. Then let each reader say her message before you validate anything for her. Were the readings similar to one another? When the client asks you his question, take a moment to just breathe and close your eyes if you need to. What thoughts come into your head? What are you sensing? Whatever comes in, whether it's your own experience or something you don't understand, it is part of the reading.

I recently provided a reading for a client who asked me about her career. I immediately thought of the fact that I held a real estate license in Massachusetts (where I'd previously lived) and was thinking about getting my license in the state I live in now, Minnesota. The client had just told me she'd moved recently from another state, and after the thought about the real estate license came into my head, I said, "Do you have a real estate license, or something like it, that you had out there that you need to get here?"

The client confirmed for me that she'd been a licensed therapist and was in the process of getting licensed in her new state.

In another instance, a client asked me for a general reading. When I tuned in for that client, I kept seeing in my head a picture of a heart with wings that I used to draw when I was a little girl. I now associate that picture with Archangel Michael. I almost didn't say it because I could not be certain of the message that was to come from that. I kept wondering why on Earth I was seeing that picture of me being a seventh grader drawing a heart with wings all over one of my folders in a classroom. The information persisted, so I eventually said, "Did you used to draw hearts with wings on everything when you were a child?"

The client gasped and said, "How did you know!"

I then told her that the drawing also symbolized Archangel Michael, and that meant that there was an archangel that was always close to her.

Basically, a reading is usually what your ego thinks is your imagination. When you have the intention of doing a reading, you are creating a sacred space for that reading and that reading alone. Any thoughts you think, whether about your own life or the reading, are part of that reading. Also, if you start a reading and find you have a hard time opening up or feel blocked and/or frustrated when you are trying to get information, it's still part of the reading. It is probably the way the situation is that they are asking about is. Maybe they feel blocked or trapped and don't know where to go. They might be unsure of their future. You can even say something like, "I'm feeling really blocked and frustrated right now, does this makes sense to you?"

Once, I was doing a reading for someone in a group setting. I can't even remember the question that was asked, but I remember seeing something that I didn't understand.

I didn't feel it pertained to the reading at all, but I had to say it anyway. In that instance, I kept seeing a kitchen cupboard open and some powdered sugar being pulled out. I had absolutely no idea what that meant, but I said it. The person I was reading for gasped and said she had been cooking with powdered sugar the day before. We don't have to know why it came up, and probably she doesn't either. Maybe it's just a way of confirming her guide's presence to her.

I have had two times where I've received a reading from different psychics where they mention the flower peony. It's my favorite flower, and somehow peonies are sacred to me. Both times I have gasped in surprise and was overcome with the affirmation that my spiritual team is around me and loves me. Sometimes that's the case when odd details get that specific and the client doesn't seem to know what it means. They just need evidence that their spiritual team is there, or of the support from the universe.

It may not be that easy to trust the information that you receive at first, but you can do this. You were born to do this. Part of doing the reading is facing the fear that you won't do this right. And the louder your ego is yelling, "You aren't good enough!" the bigger your purpose is in doing this. There is no right or wrong. Yes, it's scary to be wrong sometimes, but there is no reward without risk. You're doing this to help the client, so all you can do is say what you receive. The worst that can happen is the client won't resonate with the information at first.

Always stand firm to the information you receive and relay. Your clients may not recognize it at the time it's received, and that's okay if they don't understand it. It does not, however, mean that you are wrong. You aren't making this up, and you aren't wrong, despite the fact that your client may at some times rattle you. If your client says, "That's not right," or doesn't seem to understand what you are saying, ask her to write it down for later because it may not make sense to her now but will in the future. The chances are good that you still have had several specific hits of information (meaning that which your client easily recognizes), and will either validate instantly by their reaction—a gasp, a cry, or just the pure validation of saying, "Yes, that's right."

I am not saying that all of your readings will be like that. The majority of the time your clients will be very appreciative of the messages that you, and only you, can deliver to them. Those are the moments that affirm why I am doing this, and they will likely do the same for you.

I am not a person that does a reading and asks for much explanation beforehand. The less you know about a client going in to a reading, the better. If you start the reading and the client starts to tell you a story, try to politely ask them not to feed you information. It allows you to more easily believe and relay the messages you are receiving, and most of the information you relay will be easily validated by the client.

I have had clients that at times have seem disappointed with the information they receive initially, only to validate for me later that it was one of the best readings they have had, or how later on they realized the information was right. You may not always get the validation you seek from a client immediately, but remember you are just the messenger. If you are doing this to help someone, that's all that really is important. Find ways to ask throughout the reading, "Does that make sense to you?" Let the client say yes or no, and then move on. If you require a story in an effort to know the details of a message before continuing, it could otherwise taint the reading with information the client is giving you.

You will learn more about yourself with each reading that you do. You will learn how your guides communicate with you, and you will get better at it every time. Be patient with yourself and know that, as with anything, it takes time to grow as an intuitive or psychic reader. I remember how intimidated I used to be by some of my peers. I thought that I was never going to get it. I have evolved over the last few years, and so will you. You will never know unless you try, though. It is part of your soul's purpose to be doing this work in service to others, and that is what has led you to try to understand it more.

You are not expected to be perfect. Remember, when we are in the space of a reading, spirit does the work for us. Everything that we do or say is coming from spirit, source, the universe, God, or whatever term you prefer. You are doing this in service to others. Be gentle with yourself. You are so important to this planet right now and truly were born to do this.

NOTES

NOTES

CHAPTER 13

HOW DO I KNOW IF I'M A MEDIUM?

Have you always felt intrigued by the thought of mediums or ghosts? Have you had moments in your life where you think you saw a spirit or even just a flash of unexplained movement out of the corner of your eye?

You probably have always just *known* that there were ghosts near or around you. You may feel a chill, goose bumps, or tingling that is reminiscent of the hair standing up on your arms or back of your neck. Sometimes you may feel a sensation such as a sudden spot of cold air in an otherwise warm room. You may sometimes smell something out of thin air, like a smell that you used to notice on someone you knew, a perfume your grandmother used to wear, or the smell of a cigar that your father used to smoke.

You are somewhat obsessed with the paranormal. You watch all of the ghost hunting shows or anything you can find about ghosts, mediums, or anything paranormal. You cannot get your hands on enough about mediums or ghosts and are always seeking a new book that tells you something you did not know before. You always wish for another book that answered the questions that the last book didn't.

The thought of ghosts probably intrigues you and probably also terrifies you sometimes, too. What you DO know is that it always feels like there's just something else there. You may still sleep with a nightlight on or leave the TV on all night because you sense there is something or someone in the room with you. You may even dread the thought of going to sleep or getting sleepy because you seem to notice more paranormal activity at night, particularly in bed. And the thought of opening your eyes from sleep in a pitch black bedroom is scary because you never know what you will see or feel in the room with you. It's highly likely that you feel like no matter what you do, there are always ghosts around you. You absolutely cannot believe that you keep buying ghost-infested homes. Everywhere you go there are ghosts; you just can't seem to get away from them. Why?

You have always just known you were different. If you told anyone about the fact that you might see or sense ghosts, they'd surely lock you up or think you insane. You have tried to ignore the fact that you were a medium, but somehow the spirits always find you and pester you anyway. Sometimes you feel like they just KNOW you can sense them and will go out of their way to do things that get your attention. You can tell they're near when the hair on the back of your neck stands up or you get goose bumps. You probably argued with or denied to anyone that you were a medium. You may have said, "That's crazy!" and denounced mediums in some way.

If you have just read this passage and nodded in agreement at many of the statements, cried tears of relief that someone else understands, or exclaimed, "Yes! That's

Me!" to any of the statements, then you are a medium. You agreed to come to Earth to help others with your gift. You are one of the few special souls that have the capacity to connect others with the loved ones that they so dearly miss.

I used to wonder how the heck I could help with this gift, and I would SCREAM at anyone who tried to tell me I was a medium. I thought it was a curse. Later, when I saw how much I helped my clients after a reading by using something I had been able to do my whole life, I realized it was a special blessing to help another with my work as a medium.

So whether it thrills you or scares you, whether you feel it's a blessing or a curse, you are indeed a medium. And you are very needed on Earth right now. You do not need to be perfect to help others. You are loved, you exude love, and you are perfect just as you are right now. Everything will happen exactly as it should, so trust that Heaven has heard your prayers and your concerns. The time is now for you to open yourself up to this gift.

NOTES

CHAPTER 14

HOW TO DO A MEDIUM READING

You may not realize this, but you already have all the tools necessary to do readings. You probably do readings of some form every day and don't even know it. My mom doesn't think she's a medium. But she'll say things like "there are fourteen dead people in this room right now." So if it helps you right away NOT to think of yourself as a medium, that's okay. You'll get there one step at a time. What's important is that you do the work in service to others, not what you call yourself or how you get there. You were born with the knowledge, and now it's just up to you to recall it.

I started this journey as a frustrated medium. I knew I was a medium, but I had no idea how to use the tools I had, let alone how it could benefit others. At that time, I had a belief that I should be able to see ghosts with my naked eye. Now, I know that is possible but have since realized it would probably be too much for me to see dead people standing around me all the time.

I spent more time frustrated. No matter what I tried, I

couldn't see the spirits. I didn't realize that I was already intuiting them in other ways, in what I sensed and felt. But still, I wanted to see them. In one of my psychic classes, I asked a peer why I couldn't see them. The peer that did the reading said, "Lisa, they are standing right in front of your face waving their arms around trying to get your attention."

It was later that I realized that I was not seeing them because of the concrete idea I'd created of how I was supposed to see them. Trying to control the outcome was ultimately limiting my capacity to connect with the spirits at all.

It was not until I had a teacher who saw the same things I did that I realized I'd known how all along. It just happened differently than I'd imagined. In fact, it didn't happen until I started to imagine them. I realized they came to me just like a daydream would. Someone would ask me to contact a deceased loved one, and sometimes I would see them in my mind's eye, as most would think a product of their imagination or a dream.

Beginner Exercise

Find a friend or volunteer to be your *client*. It may be easier for you to close your eyes.

Now, who do you feel is around your client? Here are some questions to ask (not out loud to your client, rather in your head to yourself or the dead person):

- Is the energy male or female?

- Does the spirit feel young or old?

- Do they feel like a parent, friend, sibling or other?

You may feel more than one presence of a deceased loved one around your client. That's okay. Just find one to focus on the first time. You will want to verify the information you receive with your client. You can ask, "Has your father passed?" Or you might say, "You lost your father, correct?"

It can be scary to do your first time, but you will feel good when it's done because it's part of your purpose. When I get any sort of stage fright during a reading, whether it's one-on-one or on stage with a crowd, I just remember that it's not about me being right or wrong. I am just the medium who helps the dead connect with the living, and I am honored to be able to help the people that have sought my service to connect to their loved ones that have passed.

When I went to my first class as a medium student, it turned out it was a class to teach us to do platform readings. On stage. If I would have known that going in, I am not sure I would have had the courage to go! It ended up being a great experience, and I tell you this because many of you will be called to do something similar.

I learned in a recent class for experienced mediums that many mediums receive their information via *download* before they actually do the reading. In the instance that they don't have enough information to provide all the elements of the reading needed from that download, they have to see if they can get more information.

I never know how I'm going to do my readings until they occur. I realize that most of them are an initial download, but I can then get more information to translate either from the dead person, or intuitively, if needed. If you find that it's hard for you to get more than one initial download, it may help you to try to develop your psychic senses as well. All mediums are psychics, and you have this ability even if you have not developed it yet.

I also have a background of being on stage through musical performance and public speaking. I now realize that my past experience helps me when I'm onstage as a medium. If you don't have any experience with public speaking and the thought of doing public readings terrifies you, relax. You may want to start with one-on-one readings. If you are considering even small public gatherings and have no confidence with public speaking, one resource to assist could be Toastmasters, International, a nonprofit organization to assist with public speaking skills.

The Four Elements of a Medium Reading

1. **Confirmation:** Who is the person? What is their relationship to your client?

2. **Evidence:** What evidence can the spirit you are reading for provide to verify that it's really them to your client? Why are they coming through?

3. **Message of Love:** What do they want to say to your client? I love you? I'm sorry?

4. **Summarize**: Confirm to your client the information you have received to, in essence, close the reading. For example, "So, your father died of a heart attack. He always sang to you when you were a little girl and called you 'Pumpkin.' He wants you to know he loves you and will never leave you."

Confirmation

Who is it that you are speaking to? Does the presence feel male or female? Or it could be fatherly, sisterly, etc. If you want to verify the name for your client, ask the spirit to provide their name for you. Trust that if the information is supposed to come forth, the spirit coming through will provide it.

Verify for your client, "You lost your father, correct?" Or you could ask, "Has your father passed?"

Evidence

We do not choose which dead people we talk to, they choose us. Make the spirit that wishes to make contact do the work in providing evidence that will make sense to your client so that they know it is the actual person's spirit that is there.

Often times when I start a reading, I validate information about the client's appearance. Usually, I do this when I see the dead person as if they are in their favorite surrounding. Sometimes it's indoors, like in a kitchen or a home. Sometimes it's outdoors at a lake. I often see mothers and grandmothers standing in the kitchen. It usually tells me that not only did she like to cook, but she was the center of love for her home.

Sometimes I see them outdoors. I did one reading where I said, "Did your brother have a lake he liked or like the outdoors?" I asked because I saw him sitting by a lake like he was relaxing and finding a moment of peace. The client confirmed that was correct.

You may receive evidence that you will not know how to translate, but tell your client what you are getting even if you don't know what it means. It's your job to deliver the evidence, not understand it. I had another medium connect with my grandfather, and she asked, "Why does he keep showing me an angel?"

I said, "He used to call me 'Angel Face.'"

It brought tears to my eyes to hear that, and it was my way of knowing that it was truly my grandfather she was connecting with.

I was recently connecting with the deceased mother of two sisters who were in the audience of a medium panel I was on. I saw a big church organ. I said, "Was your mother a religious woman?"

They laughed and nodded yes. I said, "Well, she's telling me that she sees that you don't go to church enough."

They continued laughing and said, "Yes, that's her."

I don't know how I knew that; I just knew. If I would have not mentioned it, I would not have validated for them that it was indeed their mother I was speaking to.

It's good to remember that, when you are doing a medium reading, your spiritual teams pulls information from your own experiences as a way to communicate with you. Once I was doing a reading, and I heard a Stevie Wonder song in my head during the whole reading. That was fairly normal for me to hear a song like that in my head because I love Stevie Wonder. So, I thought nothing of it for most of the reading. When I finally said, "I'm hearing 'You are the Sunshine of My Life'" to the client, she cried and said it was a song her deceased father used to sing to her.

Remember, anything you sense (hear, see, think, feel or even taste) during a reading is part of the reading. It is your job to deliver the message. You do not have to be perfect right away. But the more you do it, the better that you will become at translating the details that may be from your own experiences. You will become better at this in a way that's translatable to your client and helps validate information for them.

If you feel like you want more evidence for your client, you can always ask the spirit to step closer into your space. Not jump into your body, but to allow their energy to merge with yours. It may allow you to imitate the way the spirit spoke or some of the spirit's bodily movements. After I had delivered a reading for a family at an event, I later went up to them and spoke more about their family member that came through in the reading. One of them said, "You are standing exactly the way she used to stand with her arms crossed! Every picture we have, she has her arms crossed like that."

You can also ask the spirit questions to provide more evidence, such as:

- How did you die?

- How old were you when you passed?

- What was your occupation?

- Did you have specific bodily markings such as tattoos, scars, or birthmarks?

- Where are you buried?

- Did you have pets?

It's okay to ask the spirit questions in order to provide more evidence. The spirit is the one that wants to connect with the person who is sitting for you, and part of establishing that connection is providing evidence of the person for whom they have lost.

Message of Love

Our deceased loved ones always have a message of love for our clients. It can be something as simple as "I love you," and frankly, in my experience, it usually is. They may show a bouquet of flowers, which to me can also mean "I love you." You may hear "I'm sorry" because of a hurt that the loved one has caused in life or just feel a certain message to give to your client (such as "I love you," which again is still what I hear the majority of the time).

Once, I had a medium call on me out of a crowd. She was linking with one of my deceased uncles. She had already provided me lots of evidence of who he was. Then she said, "Are you Native American? Because he said not to stop learning about the Native American side of the family and is proud of you for doing so."

I started to cry. I didn't know that he knew, and it meant a lot to me to hear. To me, it was such an amazing message of love. It was also an affirmation that our deceased loved ones are with us even after they go.

Usually, the messages of love I hear are limited to a statement or two such as "I love you." I used to have this idea in my head that I wasn't doing something right because I wasn't able to relay a conversation or anecdotes like I hear some other mediums do. That's when I realized that I wasn't other mediums, I was ME, and I am doing this exactly the way I am supposed to be doing it.

If you have trouble hearing anything, ask the deceased loved one for a specific message for your client. If that doesn't work, then ask your spiritual team for help with it. Sometimes they may not wish to say anything at all. When they do not say anything, the message is sometimes that the loved one coming through was the silent type when they were here, and they haven't changed on the other side. At times, the message is just as simple as "I love you." Try not to worry if it is not a lengthy message. Trust the information you are receiving and that it's right for your client.

Remember, no two readings are the same. There are times when I have even read for the same client and connected with a deceased loved one more than once. One time the deceased loved one didn't say much; the other time he said more than I would have expected. As in life, sometimes our departed loved ones are talkative, and sometimes they're not.

Summarize

At the end of the reading, summarize all that you have brought through from their deceased loved one during the reading. For instance, "We spoke to your father who was in his fifties when he passed suddenly of a heart attack. He loved golf and always took you for ice cream on Friday nights. He said he loved you, and he is sorry he left so fast. He's okay now and free of his pain."

Reading Spirits by Position

One thing that may help you when you are beginning is to imagine that all the spirits have a certain position in relation to your client's body.

On your client's left side is the paternal side of the family, the father's side. The closer the relationships are, the closer they are to the client's head. For instance, a dad will look like he's right behind the client or his head may seem almost over your client's shoulder. A paternal grandpa will seem like he's sitting on the shoulder and so forth. You will likely intuit a fatherly energy. So say it's an uncle who's on the father's side but is standing where you'd normally see a father. Maybe the uncle was like a father figure.

On your client's right side is the maternal side of the family, the mother's side. In addition to maternal relatives, there can be anyone and everyone else such as friends, lovers and pets on the mother's side. Those non-familial relationships are likely out a bit farther than the mom's family would be. Say they will stand on the mom's side but further out at elbow length, if you will. As with the father's side, I always see mothers like they are right behind the client's ear or in the crook of the client's neck. Maternal grandparents look like they are on a shoulder. Great-grandparents stand slightly behind the grandparents, and aunts and uncles stand further out to what I would equate with being the upper arm (with arms outstretched). If there are deceased brothers and sisters, they usually stand in the area of the upper arm, as well.

If your client was adopted, they will always have one member of their biological family standing with them, regardless of if they ever knew or met them. I always see that person as standing directly behind the client, and I can usually intuit that in some way the person doesn't fit with the other family. I know someone that was adopted from Russia, and she has her Russian paternal great-grandfather standing behind her, even though she has never met her biological family.

Babies and Children

There are two ways in which you will see babies and children on the other side in relation to your client. If your client has ever lost a child, which could mean actually having a child that died, even through miscarriage or abortion, you will see the child present in the space under the arm on the client's maternal side. Imagine a mother with her children close to her and her arm around them.

That's usually the space in which you see those children. You may also see children that have also died with another relative in the reading, such as your client's father holding a child. The children that you see in this space are the children that were lost, and those children are not coming back to them in this lifetime. They stay near their mother as a comfort to them both, but if they walk near her, they are not coming back in this lifetime. The babies or children that have yet to be born appear in a different way called baby bubbles.

Baby Bubbles

Clients that are of child-bearing age, or who wish to have a child, whether male or female, usually have baby bubbles around their head. It means that you will actually intuit definite bubbles above the crown of your client's head. I usually see these bubbles clairvoyantly as being blue or pink, which tells me if it will be a girl or boy. I also tend to see an infant reflected in the baby bubble. In the instances of an older child that comes through adoption or some other way to the parent, I tend to see an older child reflected as a face in the baby bubble, as well. If you can't see, don't worry; you will obtain this information in whichever way you are most comfortable.

Baby bubbles are changeable, depending on the choices that your client makes. For instance, I had one client that had two blue baby bubbles, but one on each side of her head. Each baby bubble was attached to a different father, so that meant that both babies would likely not come at the same time. This depended on her life choices (and who knows, if she doesn't choose either *father*, will she have either of those babies at all?). It's important to remember that every reading says something about the future that is changeable based on the client's choices.

Final Details About Medium Readings

How do you turn this ability *off?* I have been asked this question several times. Before I learned how to use this gift, I felt like there were dead people everywhere and that they sometimes chased me. Once I started to learn how to use it, I gained the ability to call upon the gift during the space of a reading or readings. There are still times when I sense them around, particularly if I am tired and my human defenses are down. We are mediums. There will always be dead people around us. They tend to honor us more when we begin to honor them through learning how to deliver messages to their loved ones through our readings. Try to be patient with yourself as you develop as a medium. This gift cannot be forced. You already have the gift, and now it's just a matter of allowing yourself the time and space to develop. You don't have to be like any other medium; you are perfect just as you are.

NOTES

NOTES

CHAPTER 15

WHEN READINGS GO WRONG

Not every reading you do will leave you feeling great. Sometimes you will have a reading that is fabulous—both for your client and for you. One of the best things you could possibly have is a client that validates everything that you bring through for him or her. Unfortunately, not every sitter is like that.

It's really hard when you have a person that is sitting for your message and he or she looks at you with a stare that holds no acknowledgement whatsoever. It's okay to ask your client, "Do you understand that?" You may even add "yes or no" to the end of the statement if the person is still not acknowledging your message in a way that gives you the information you need to keep going.

I have noticed that there are times when I'm doing readings as a medium, particularly if my client has lots of deceased family or loved ones, that I may bring through a person other than who the client wants to hear from. I have heard many of my peers and teachers that are mediums say that they can't always pick who comes through. That is sometimes true. When a client wants to bring through his or her mother, bringing through another person may visibly disappoint your client. If you are getting another person that's coming through, stay with it for a minute or two. That deceased person may bring the one through from whom your client really wants to hear. This sometimes happens.

I used to trade readings with a lady that I knew. The readings I provided for her were always emotionally heavy. She suspected her husband might have been cheating and, no matter how many readings we did, the question stayed the same. Through the majority of the readings, the answer was no (he was not cheating). One day the answer was yes. Imagine how she felt. She'd started the reading wanting the truth, and her guides brought it through for her. That doesn't mean that the truth was easy to hear. She got off the phone crying. I got off the phone crying. That call with her helped me decide that bringing through that kind of information to my clients is not for me.

It's okay for you to renegotiate a part of your soul contract for giving readings as you evolve as a reader. That's what I did after that reading with my friend made us both feel awful. I announced to my guides that I did not want to be the reader that brought through that information and that if a client needed that to please direct him or her to someone else that could give that client what he or she needed.

In my work as a psychic medium, I am sometimes asked questions that make me as the reader uncomfortable. I've been asked by several clients, "When will my Grandma die?" or something similar. I've recently adopted a policy in telling clients that I won't answer questions like that. Just because someone comes to you and is paying for your service does not mean that you have to tell them something that makes you uncomfortable. It's okay to say no.

When you are getting immense detail about a client in a reading, use your discretion as to how to relay the message. Yes, everything you get is part of the reading. That being said, please be considerate of your clients. Telling your client every gruesome detail of the way their loved one passed may not always be the best idea when they've already suffered a horrific loss.

On the business side of giving readings, I do a lot of psychic fair events. This is where there may be several other psychics, mediums, or readers at one event, and we all share space for a day where people can come out to see us and perhaps stop for a reading. I was doing one such event, and a woman came in near the end of the day. Before we started the reading, she told me that she had driven a long way to come to the event that day. The reading evolved like a conversation that started off on the wrong foot. She told me that every message I brought through was too general and dismissed the information. Hearing that continually for several minutes allowed doubt to seep into my being. That doubt may have blocked whatever information was coming through, but finally I said to her, "This is not working for you, is it?"

She said that it wasn't. When she said that, I told her I was not going to charge her for the reading. I told her that such things sometimes happen, and we hugged each other at the end of it. At that event, there were plenty of other readers there, and hopefully she got the message she was looking for. It was just not me that was supposed to be giving that message to her that day.

That experience taught me something. I had never had an experience like that in all of the readings I'd given. Sure, some were better than others, but never had I been inclined to think it wasn't worth giving to the point of a refund. I just knew in my heart that day it was the right thing to do. Some of my peers say that whether they can bring a message through or not they still charge the client. If you feel like that, too, it's your business and you can absolutely make your own policy. I feel that it's kind to give them a refund if I can't bring a message through. In this business, our reputation is everything, and I don't want to be known for being the person that takes money even when I can't bring a message through.

After that failed reading, I felt bad. I doubted myself and wondered what the purpose of that failure was. I didn't let it get to me enough to never do a reading again, of course. I eventually knew that I had that experience to realize that I'm not always perfect and that the message isn't always perfect. Sometimes I may not be able to bring a message through, and I won't always know why. The only thing I can do about that is to try to learn from it and know I didn't do anything wrong. Perhaps it was just not me that was supposed to deliver the message, and I have to trust that.

When I do psychic fairs, I can sit down and do back-to-back readings all day long. At some point in the day, I may be exhausted and know that I have hit the wall, so to speak, with my capacity to provide readings. I can choose whether or not I want to continue giving readings in an exhausted state or not. If I do, the clients that come to me after that may not get the evidence I could provide in earlier readings, and usually I stop when I feel like that. Recently, I had one of my peers come to me and bring me her sister for a reading near the end of the day at an event like that. It was such an honor that she'd trust me with her sister, but I had to say no because it was late in the day and I'd hit my limit with readings. My peer understood and thanked me for telling her.

Not all of your readings will be perfect. Most of them will be wonderful both for you and for your client. When they aren't good readings, just know that it's a part of the business for that to happen and that you are still good at what you do even when you have a reading that is off.

NOTES

CHAPTER 16

CHANNELING

Ah, the great mystery of channeling. You might have different ideas of what you think it is or is not. The very thought of it might scare you or intrigue you. My personal thought of channeling now does not differ too much from when I first started hearing about it. To me, it is when another spirit talks through your body. There are those who may think it is possession, which is a subject I do not give energy to; I only place energy in the positive and pray for protection when it comes to channeling and helping my clients.

When I first really heard of it, beyond scary movies, was in one of my psychic development classes. The teacher told stories of the various times she was doing medium readings and other spirits or beings popped into her body and channeled messages through her. I could tell in the way she spoke about it that it was not always a pleasant experience for her. It was at that precise moment that I decided that there was no way I was ever doing that. When I started doing readings, I did not start channeling right away. After a while, channeling evolved in a way that was customized for me. I think I had the idea that I would completely step out of my body, letting the spirit takeover. Honestly, I still feel that I need to be in control.

I did not realize that I would be present during channeling. I would be in my body while a different voice talked through me. It took a while for me to figure out what was going on. First, I realized that there were times when I could not remember the details of some readings. I compared this loss of memory to my ability to recollect in readings at which I knew I was present, and the readings were somehow different. Then, I realized I had never heard voices like I'd hear while I was channeling. At first I thought I was making it up, but then I pieced together that I was channeling. I have asked Archangel Michael to protect me in all things. I trust that he protects me and will not let another channel messages through me unless they are safe for me and for the client to whom the messages are meant.

One night I gave a reading to a friend who is also a peer of mine in the psychic world. He always calls himself a skeptic. So, I suppose that it was apropos that his guides chose to channel the majority of his reading. They sounded nothing like me and said things to him that he knew I did not know. I remember him looking up in surprise at me, almost as if he wanted to check to see if it still was me.

I usually do not know when I am going to channel. As I said, I just trust my guides and Archangel Michael to protect me at all times. It usually happens subtly, but it totally depends on the guide or spirit that I am channeling. Some spirits have stronger energy than others, just like humans. I can consciously hear that my voice changes, yet I know I have the power to stop it at any time. I am always doing it from the loving space of a reading and do not usually stop it. Sometimes I go back and forth about wanting to be able to talk in my own voice, and so the actual reading occasionally sounds like two different people in the same sentence and somewhat strained as a result. Sometimes they channel first and then let me talk second. Maybe it's because they can't find the message they want to deliver in the database that is my brain or just because they want to speak directly to the client for some reason.

So how is that? Clear as mud? I tell you this to try to explain it from the best of my ability. I do not know how I do it; I just do it. I recommend you only try channeling after asking for the protection of your guides and the angels, as I do. I also have the intention that every one of my readings is a positive experience for both me and the client, and it usually is. I also recommend that you first try to deliver readings without channeling and ask your guides to work it into the reading if it is for your greatest and highest good and that of your client. Ask them to do it in a way that is right for you. That way, it can be a little more gradual and natural. At the beginning of my readings, I sometimes explain how it works to my clients. I know when I feel like making a disclosure to my clients, the odds are good that I may channel during the reading, and then I usually do.

There is another kind of channeling that is done through writing. Some may think of it as automatic writing. I used to become frustrated wondering how to do that. I have learned that I am able to do this one step at a time through my journey. I have channeled messages from Archangel Michael, and, when I do, I can feel his energy around me as I write. They are generally not long messages, but I can feel his energy, if you will, and know that it is not me giving the message when I do. How do I know, you ask? I just know and trust that the information I am feeling is correct.

In a class that I teach, we usually do readings on each other, and in this setting we write our readings down. I usually don't do this type of reading, except for the occasional email reading and the class I facilitate. Sometimes, when I get done writing the reading, I notice that my handwriting is sloppy and wonder where it's coming from. One day, at the end of the reading I had written, I handed the paper to the girl the reading was for. She started to cry and said, "That's my DAD'S handwriting."

I had no idea I was channeling it when I did it, but I knew it was someone's handwriting other than my own.

If you are fascinated with channeling and how to do it, it is likely something your soul knows you are able to do. Try to let go of the *how* to do it, and trust that if it is supposed to happen it will. In that way, you stay open to the highest possible energy when doing so.

LISA ANDRES

NOTES

CHAPTER 17

GHOSTBUSTING

The Art of Crossing Over the Dead

Some of you that are mediums may also feel a call to help the dead in a way beyond providing readings to others. You've likely seen many movies and/or heard stories about buildings, homes, or places where earthbound spirits reside. With the recent popularity of shows about haunted places, it's more likely that you have. In many of these shows, they tend to want to only prove paranormal existence. What I am referring to is helping the spirits that are stuck here, so to speak, find their way home to Heaven and, at the very least, to remove them from the space.

When I do a house clearing job, I am there to help heal the dead that, for one reason or another, have been stuck on Earth. That means that I help them to heal and cross over to the light. When I first started my psychic classes, this was always something I was fascinated with. I wanted so badly to do it, but it was difficult for me to find the right teacher or opportunity to do so.

I can't remember exactly when or how I received my first

house clearing job, but now after many of them, I get referrals to do them by word of mouth. In the past, I have always had other things going on, but I just know that when I am supposed to do it, jobs will show up.

I started out doing this with one other person, my friend Emily. We would go and do the job in tandem; she would do the healing of the spirit, and I would work with Archangel Michael to cross it over. These jobs usually come with a request to clear space, so we would also do some energy clearing as well. I will take you through the way that I help a spirit to cross over. I'm sure that there are no two of us that work alike, and you will likely develop your own style as you get into this.

I work with many spiritual helpers to cross over the dead, primarily Archangel Michael. I can do these jobs both remotely and at someone's house, and most of my clients call me to their home to help them because that's where they feel the spirit(s).

When I arrive, I speak with my clients and ask what they want. Is there a specific spirit or area that they need addressed? I always want to make sure that I get their permission to do this because some people actually want the spirits there. It may sound crazy, but some people like having their visitors from the other side.

As I begin the clearing, I light palo santo wood or sage to clear the negative energy. I start going from room to room to clear them and sense what dwells there. Some rooms will feel they just need to be cleared of the sludge of energy that is there from the living. Some may feel negative and make the hair on the back of your neck stand up. Those rooms are most likely where spirits reside that are earthbounds. I do not ever ask why they are there and, as such, will not be addressing that in this book.

I then ask help from Archangel Michael and whatever other heavenly angels or ascended masters from which I feel guided. I mentally tell the spirit why I am there, and I ask it if it is ready to go. I have yet to have one tell me no. I then ask Archangel Michael to help the spirit and send it healing and watch the spirit transform like a flower that was growing from a seed. It's a beautiful process, and when it is healed, which I intuitively know (it's when it looks like that beautiful flower, if you will), I work with Archangel Michael to send it to the light. I always know and feel when it happens because I automatically feel the energy in the room change, as if a presence has just left. I have had other jobs where it was several hundred ghosts, and that is similar but less on an individual level with the spirit that's crossing over. I usually send them in groups and trust that if I am sent there to cross them, it is time for that to happen.

When you encounter such a presence, tune in to what you feel like when you are doing a medium reading. I do all of this entirely through my third eye, or what you may think of as your imagination or mind's eye. If you want to consider it your imagination, the ghost and all that occurs with the crossing is whatever it is you are imagining. What you are imagining is usually clairvoyant information. Very little of the actual process is out loud, if you will, and it is in co-creation with God and the angels.

Then, start talking to the spirit, and ask if they are ready to go home. They usually are, or you wouldn't have been called there. Then ask Archangel Michael to come in to assist you in helping this spirit cross over to the light. Ask for healing of this (dead) person, and watch how its presence evolves from heavy to bright and light. When this occurs, ask Archangel Michael to help carry this soul to the light.

I had a job where I was called to a woman's home because she thought she had a ghost and also wanted an energy clearing. As my friend and I went to do the job, we remarked about the neighborhood and how many *dead people* were looking through windows of the neighboring homes as we walked by.

When we arrived, we spoke with the client and then proceeded to go from room to room, clearing the space. When we got near her front porch, I sensed the spirit of a male in his thirties. It was a presence that had heavier energy from a lifetime of alcoholism. I could sense this because of not only the actually heavy feeling of the spirit, but also because he was covered with a pallor that was almost ashen in presentation. There are some earthbound spirits that stick around to feed their addictions from other humans that have the same addiction.

I asked the client, "Do you drink a lot, or go to bars?"

She said, "I used to."

I then proceeded to tell her about the soul that was stuck there. The spirit likely followed her around from her drinking days and probably still waited for the day that she'd take a drink again so he could feed his addiction.

My friend and I set to work in the client's home. We spoke to the spirit and let him know why we were there. Emily started to channel this spirit healing. His aura and presence went from what I perceived as ashen (almost like soot on him) to light and bright—his energy lifted like the bright sun. It was then I knew he was ready, and I asked Archangel Michael to please carry him home. My friend and I both got teary-eyed as we felt his energy leave the room and go home to Heaven.

As I have evolved in some of the jobs I've done, I notice that a lot of my work starts the minute the appointment is booked. I have not had jobs that take me all day. Stylistically, I do these jobs just as I would approach anything in life. I dive in and get the job done, for the most part, quite efficiently. I've wondered at times if clients expect more hocus pocus from me, but that's not what I'm about.

As I've noted, when I do a job to help a spirit cross over, or a house clearing, I always ask Archangel Michael to protect me. He is a universal, omnipresent Archangel, which means he can be several places at once. He will always help any who ask him. So, before I start a reading, I say, "Archangel Michael, please be with me and protect me. Help me to only speak or channel messages of love for this client that are to the greatest highest and good of all concerned." I have complete faith that when I ask he will protect me, and he does. Remember, angels can only help if you ask; they have a contract to respect our free will and, for the most part, that means that they do not help unless we ask.

In a house, I often ask for several angels to be posted at the doors and windows, to protect it, and I always ask for Archangel Michael to clear it and cut the fear-based energy cords. There are many homes with dense energy, and that really helps to clear it.

I also often call on the Celtic goddess, Dana. She helps me with furniture by clearing energy out of furniture. When we sit on or sleep on something daily, such as a sofa or a bed, it absorbs all of our energy, good or bad. Many of us pick up other energies when we are out, so at times we unintentionally bring lesser energies home with us. Dana helps to clear that out of furniture.

I also often call on the goddess Isis to help me when I am crossing other spirits over to the light because she is a goddess associated with past lives. She is a great aide at my side when I ask. She is powerful and can help shield me and help me to facilitate the crossing over of spirits.

Once I see a spirit cross over, I know that I have helped another child of God find its way home. That's one of the reasons I am on Earth. If you have just read this passage, it may be part of your purpose to be involved in ghost busting in some way.

Orbs

Orbs are circular objects that appear in photos. Have you ever had a picture taken where you didn't see anything in the room with your eye, but then when you saw the picture, there seemed to be one or several circular objects on or around you?

Orbs can be several things. They could be as simple as dust or rain. Sometimes orbs are more than that. When orbs appear to have a texture to them, they are likely some sort of spirit presence. I would say that, for the most part, you have to use your intuition to figure out what it might be.

It might be a traditional ghost, it could be one of your spirit guides, or it could even be an angel. If you see an orb that seems to have color to it, that is usually an angel. Look at the color codes associated with archangels, and that can usually tell you what kind of angel has appeared.

NOTES

CHAPTER 18

YOUR SPIRITUAL TEAM: YOUR GUIDES, ANGELS , AND OTHER ESOTERIC HELPERS

We all come to Earth with a spiritual team. Yes, a team. For everyone it's different. While I have had many people ask me who their spirit guide was in readings , in many instances they have more than one guide. Lightworkers tend to have entire teams of angels, spirit guides and other ascended masters. At times, there are animals, faeries and more.

The first time I actually heard one of my *guides* being called out was when a friend of mine in college, who was a psychic, said "Whoa, you're Native American, aren't you?"

I looked around to try to understand what she was seeing, but then said, "Well, yes, I have Native American ancestry; how did you know?"

She said, "Because everyone I have ever met that is Native American has tons of Native American spirit guides around them, and you walked in here with several flanking you on both sides."

I was floored! I learned that evening that my primary Native American guide is named Dancing Flame. Since then, I have also learned that he is my protector and always by my side to make sure I am safe. He was my father in another life and signed on to protect me in this one.

There are some guides that come with us, such as a guardian or protector, which are here to be with us for our entire human life. Some guides also come in temporarily for certain things such as only for our childhood, or perhaps a scholar or teacher of some sort that helps us with our education. The bottom line is this: we all have at least one spirit guide of some sort and one angel that are with us for our entire life. There are likely many others, too.

There's a very good chance that you have spent one or more of your lifetimes as a spirit guide. Imagine how frustrating it must be for our guides when we, their charges, don't listen to their messages. One reason we probably came to Earth as lightworkers is because we are more likely to be heard when we are here in the flesh. When we sit down with all of those whom we make contact with in this life, we also contact many of our spirit guides. There's more about that in the Akashic records section of this book.

What I have learned over the years is that I have a pack of guides—lots of them. Chances are that you do, too. That's common for lightworkers. I have Native Americans, angels (Archangel Michael), ascended masters (such as Isis and Merlin), power animals and many of my deceased loved ones from this life, including some that I've never met because they died before I was born. If you have someone in your family you were named after that is now deceased, there is a very good chance that person is one of the guides amongst your spiritual team.

I have encountered a group of my guides through another psychic that channels them when I have a reading with her. I always had an image of Shakespearean times when she spoke of them. I could not see explicit detail but always felt that their clothing was of that time. Usually, I had a hard time understanding their messages. That's when they told me and affirmed that they were from that time period. Language has changed since then, so they had to work to find words I could understand.

Since I have opened up psychically and have accepted the presence of my spiritual team, I speak to them a regular basis. I don't really always have to hear them talk or answer back, but it comforts me to know they are there. Sometimes I make a statement and will intuit the answer in feeling or thought and not necessarily hear one of them speak. Or sometimes I will just ask for their assistance with something and then trust that they help.

I also have lots of faeries in my spiritual team. They don't want to be left out of this because they are with so many of you who are reading this. Faeries are especially around those of you who are passionate about environmental issues of any kind. They also tend to stay with people who feel they have a connection to the witch trials or who may have a past life in which they were a sorcerer, alchemist, or priestess of some kind. Many psychics, mediums, and intuitives were, in their past lives, witches who were burned at the stake during the witch trials. The faeries were there with us many times. If that resonates with you and you have a draw to faeries of any kind, that's why.

You could have dolphins, mermaids, unicorns, a shaman, or indigenous medicine man in your spiritual team. This team consists of anything you can imagine, and, if those thoughts are repetitive, that's your first clue that you have those people or things are around you in your spiritual team all the time. I once had a client ask me what her spirit guide's name was. When I told her the names of her two spirit guides I got, she said, "Oh, those are my cat's names!"

Having explained how spirit guides connect with you, I would like for you now to take a moment and make a list of the people, angels, or things that you have always had a connection to or felt were with you. Close your eyes, relax, and breathe. What is it that comes into your presence? Do you feel, see, hear, or just know a message? Whatever it is you are receiving and feel compelled to write down is part of your spiritual team. If you want, you can also ask your guide to come to you in a dream. Ask that they give you clear information that you will easily remember when you wake up. It might be a good idea to keep a notepad of some kind by your bed, as well, to write what we feel as we wake. Those are some of our most lucid times for receiving messages from the universe.

When you start to allow yourself to receive and hear more psychic information, you will start to receive more information about your guides. The best thing to know for now is that they are always there for you. So, even if you can't hear them, they can hear you. They like it when you speak to them. So tell them your request or concerns; ask them for help. Then, trust that the repetitive thoughts or signs that you receive are from your guides because they probably are!

In the past, I would sometimes voice my anger and frustration to my spirit guides about certain things. I once apologized to them for being so rude to them sometimes. In response, they said the most loving thing to me. My spirit guides answered, "That's okay! We love you and knew exactly who you were and what we were signing up for when we came to be with you, and we would not have you any other way."

It's very likely your spiritual team feels the same way about you!

NOTES

CHAPTER 19

HOW TO IDENTIFY
YOUR SPIRITUAL TEAM

The best way to identify parts of your spiritual team is to define the things to which you are drawn. Here is a list that may help you through this process.

Fairies

If you are drawn to faeries (including having a love of Disney's TinkerBell), work with the outdoors or nature in any way, or believe you have a connection to the witch trials and/or Salem, you likely have several faeries on your spiritual team.

Mermaids

If you are drawn to the ocean or mermaids (including Disney's Ariel) and sometimes have dreams about being a mermaid, you likely have mer-people (people from the sea) in your spiritual team.

Dolphins

Like mermaids, if you are drawn to the ocean and/or dolphins in any way, you likely have dolphins in your spiritual team.

Native Americans

If you are Native American and/or have a draw to shamanism and are fascinated by the Native American people and their culture, you likely have Native Americans in your spiritual team.

Merlin

If you have a draw to Avalon, magic or Merlin himself, it is likely that Merlin is one of your spiritual helpers

Angels

If you feel you always have angels around you, you do and have many in your spiritual team. When you read the chapter on archangels, feel which ones you feel drawn to. Those are likely archangels that are part of your spiritual team.

Deceased Loved Ones

Do you have deceased loved ones you are named after? Do you have a deceased loved one that you feel is around often? They are likely a part of your spiritual team.

Star People

Do you have a draw to other planets and a love of the stars? Do you often feel like you were dropped off on the wrong planet? Are you fascinated with UFOs? If you are nodding in agreement, you likely have guides from other planets watching over you lovingly.

Wise Ones

Do you feel as if you may have been a wise witch, high priestess, or sorceress? Do you possess a penetrating look that some say is always serious? You likely have many guides on your team that are wise ones and ascended masters. You will find more about these guides in the "Ascended Masters" chapter. The ones you feel most drawn to are in your spiritual team.

Time Periods

What time periods do you feel most drawn to or, conversely, hate for no reason? Is it one? Is it more than one? No matter the answer, whichever time period you feel most strongly about is the time in history from which your spiritual teams comes. You probably know them because you have spent another lifetime or lifetimes with them.

How to Hear Your Spiritual Team and Angels

Exercise

If you meditate, or wish to relax and try to see your guides, the best way to do so is to find a quiet space and lie down. Next, close your eyes and imagine yourself in a quiet, peaceful meadow. Imagine yourself walking until you find a place that looks like there is a door. Go to the door and open it. What, or who, is it that you see on the other side of that door? What does the person look like? What kind of clothes is he or she wearing? Ask the person's name. How did/do you know them? You will do this entire exercise in your head, or what you would perceive to be your imagination. That's how I receive a lot of my information, and it is the best way for you to start. There is no pressure to get all of the details at first. Just go with the first answer you get. Sometimes, you simply feel the first answer rather than hear or see it. Trust it. Ask your guide to then enter your dreams for affirmation or give you some sort of sign for affirmation. Be sure to keep a notebook near your bed so that you may write information down.

NOTES

CHAPTER 20

ANGELS

Angels are with you all of the time. You probably have believed that you have a guardian angel for some time, perhaps all of your life. We all have one. The main purpose of a guardian angel is to protect you from an untimely death. Have you had times where you felt you were miraculously saved from some sort of disaster, such as a traffic accident? Well, that was likely the intervention of your guardian angel.

What you may not know is that there are several angels around you at all times. They would love to help you with anything and everything. As humans, part of our contract on Earth is that we have free will to make our own choices during this life on Earth. What that means is that angels cannot intervene unless we ask. They love to help us, if only we ask. Now, that does not always mean you will get an instant answer, or the answer that you want, but they will always help when you actually ask.

Angels come with only love and are without judgment of any sort. Most of them have never had human lives and work for God. So if you have ever thought an angel was telling you something such as "You're bad", it wasn't an angel. Most likely that was an ego-based thought from a place of fear.

If you want to ask an angel for help, you can ask either out loud or in your head. They love it when you talk to them and tell them all your problems or your fears and desires. You can never tell too much or too little. They are with you at all times.

There are times when I say to mine, "Please take my fears about this situation (that is troubling me)."

I imagine myself lifting my arms and giving my burden to the angels. I had a broken heart a few years ago, and I knew I would be filled with sorrow and grief while I healed. Since the pain of heartbreak is so excruciating, I asked my angels to please take some of my sadness from me. I have always felt that they did.

Prior to my realization and acceptance of being a medium and a psychic, I was feeling a bit like a victim. I did not understand why I was on Earth, and I felt cynical about many things. As I drove to work one day, I was singing along to a song by Sara Bareilles called "Come Round Soon." I was singing her lyrics at the top of my lungs, "The angels said I'd smile today. Who needs angels anyway?"

I remember thinking, "Yeah, it's not like they've ever helped me anyway!"

A few months later, I received a book about angels as a gift, and it changed my life. Not only do I now believe in angels, I ask for their help in many things. When you see sparkles or mysterious flashes of color in the air around you, usually above the head, those are angels. When you see colored sparkles of light in the air, it is usually an Archangel. When you see sparkles of white light, they represent other angels such as guardian angels or angels that are with or near you.

Clients I give readings to often ask, "What angel do I have with me?" This is likely something you will get in your practice, as well. As with any reading, it is the first thing that pops into my head or first thing that I intuit. So, if I feel that it is Archangel Michael, I may say, "I feel that you have a strong connection to Archangel Michael. He is associated with the color purple. Is purple one of your favorite colors? Do you sometimes notice that you just manifest purple things around you? You might even see purple flecks or sparkles in the air at times."

The answer is almost always "yes" when that is the information I feel guided to provide. So, if you see a color that you LOVE, have everywhere, wear often, or see, possibly as the colored sparkles in the air, it is likely the archangel that you associate with most. My Grandma Ali loves, loves, loves the color purple, so what does that say about her? She has probably got Archangel Michael with her! The angels want to remind you that you can call on them anytime, for anything. No request is too big or too small. You do not have to worry about taking an archangel, or any angel, away from someone else who needs them more. Angels are omnipresent, meaning they can be with many people simultaneously.

Remember, when you ask them for assistance, you may not always receive an immediate answer. Also, they may not always answer in the way you think they should answer. The trick is to try to let go of the details and the need to understand how something is going to happen, and let it transpire with the help of the angels. You then have to trust that it will happen. The angels hear you the first time you ask, and they usually are not expecting you to ask them again. At times, it may seem like you are not receiving an answer, but it may be that your desire has not yet manifested. It is also possible that no answer, or what you perceive to be no answer, is, in fact, the answer that is for your highest good. You just may not realize it at the time, or it could be that more patience is required. Regardless, your requests to the angels do not go unanswered. It just may not be the outcome you expect.

If you want a sign that your angel is there, ask for a sign. Angels sometimes give signs in the form of coins. If you see one that is on the ground, it is usually a sign from an angel. A sign from an angel is proof of their love and that they are near you. The same can be said of feathers. Even if it is a feather from something in your home such as a down coat or pillow, it is a sign from an angel. At times, I see a vehicle pass me with a business name that has "angel" in the title or a school bus with "angel" in the name of the school. I always know that represents a sign from the angels.

Certain songs contain messages from angels. Whenever I hear these songs, I know it is a sign from my angels. In 2010, I was moving across the country (1,400 miles) to Boston, Massachusetts. When I was looking for an apartment in Boston, I was crushed for time since I was only there for a weekend. I also did not know the neighborhoods. I did not know if I would find the right place, and I was worried about it. I drove to a new neighborhood my realtor had suggested, and it felt good to me. I grew up in a Jewish neighborhood and saw a synagogue on the corner. I knew that was a sign because it made me feel at home. Then, all of the sudden, a song that I associate as being an angel message came on the radio. It had never really had radio play, yet there it was playing on my radio. I knew it was a sign from my angels, and, even though I had not pulled up to the apartment, I could not help wondering if this would be my home. Sure enough, I ended up signing a lease for that apartment, and I always knew that my angels helped me find it.

So, if you ask your angels for a sign, try to stay open and be receptive to the answer. If you hear a song and say, "I wonder if that's from my angels," it is. If you see something and wonder if that is the sign you were looking for, it is. That's your intuition telling you that it is, along with your angels. Sometimes, I see signs at random from angels when I am having a bad or dark-seeming day. One day I was rather cranky on my way to work, wondering WHY on Earth I had this long commute and had to sit in traffic, etc. As I was sitting there at a stoplight, all of the sudden, a school bus pulled up beside me that said *Academy of Holy Angels* on the side. I started to cry happy tears and knew it was a message of love and support from the angels.

One practice I have recently adopted is to ask the angels at bedtime to rearrange my thoughts so that my dreams will work to my greatest and highest good. It is important to know that you should be sober when you do this. I always wake up the next morning feeling refreshed, like I have been cleansed in a special way.

You have an extra special connection to the angels if you are always inspired to put angel-themed decor in your home or work place. If you have a tattoo of wings, you are probably part angel yourself. Remember when I said that a lightworker is also known as an Earth angel? Well, Earth angels can be part angel or have angel-like qualities. If your name is Angel, Angela, or something with "angel" in it, you definitely have a connection to angels.

Your angels are full of love for you and always by your side. They love that you are reading this and that you want to know more about angels. Just remember, your angels are only a thought away. You do not need to know who they are to ask for their help. You do not need to be Christian, or any other religion for that matter, to ask for their help. They love everyone, as they all see everyone as Love.

They are waiting for you to ask for their assistance. If you are afraid to ask, just start by thanking them for being there. You do not have to see them to do that. You can start by asking them to come to you in your dreams. You can also ask them to protect you, your house, or your loved ones at any time. Whatever it is you want to ask, there is nothing too big or too small, just ask. Even if you are not yet ready to ask them for anything, take comfort in knowing that there are always angels around us.

Archangels

Archangels are, in many ways, an extension of the hand of God. They work to carry our prayers to God and also to dispatch teams of even more angels to help answer our prayers. There are more archangels than the ones in this section, but these are the ones I felt guided to share with you and work with most often. I am listing them as a resource for you so that you can know who they are and what their specialties are. As with any angel, you may call on them for anything. This resource may help point you in the right direction if you do not know where to start.

Archangel Michael – Protector

Archangel Michael is the universal, or all-purpose, archangel. He shields and protects all who ask, and he has contracted with some to come as part of their spiritual team. He is often associated with police officers and any additional civil servants who protect others. He is with the Indigos, as they are warriors of some sort who effect positive change. He is also a wonderful resource for technology and issues that need a fix of some sort, such as help with your computer or a plumbing fix.

He also works to protect mediums, especially if they are "ghost busting." He can dispatch a squadron to help a lost soul heal and cross over to the light.

Color: Purple/Cobalt Blue

You can ask Archangel Michael to guard you at all times in all relationships and aspects of your life. He will make sure that you are safe. He wants you to know, however, if you do this, you may also lose some relationships or situations in your life that are not for your greatest and highest good. These relationships may or may not re-enter your life at a time when they are better suited for your greatest good. In many instances, his intervention helps to align your energy with those that compliment it the most, and it can also bring wonderful new relationships and situations into your life, as well.

Archangel Raphael – Healer

Archangel Raphael has green healing energy, and he is present with those that need healing or are healers. He is present on the spiritual team with all doctors and healers, whether traditional or non-traditional healers. He is also present with Crystal adults and children.

Color: Emerald Green

You can ask Archangel Raphael for healing for yourself or others that need help. You can send him to a person, even if you do not necessarily have their actual consent or knowledge, with the intention of Raphael healing the person with their soul's permission.

Archangel Gabriel – Messenger

Archangel Gabriel is the Messenger of God. He is present with all orators, whether they are involved with the spoken or written word. If you are an author or musician that creates books or music, for instance, Gabriel is with you. If you are someone that speaks to crowds in an inspirational way, Gabriel is with you. Call upon him if you wish to have a child, whether through conception or adoption. He is also present with many children. This includes crystal children and some of the Indigos.

Color: Silver and/or Gold

You can call upon Archangel Gabriel if you are looking for inspiration in your career as an author. Even if you have not started the book or work yet, he will inspire you with divine guidance, helping you successfully complete your project or reach your desired result.

Archangel Jophiel – Beauty

Archangel Jophiel is helpful when you need to call upon her to beautify your home, wardrobe, appearance, or thoughts. She is also a wonderful resource for clearing energy in homes. If you clear homes in any way, such as with Feng Shui, interior design, or even in helping clear earthbound spirits from homes, call upon Archangel Jophiel for help.

Color: Hot Pink

You can call on Archangel Jophiel to clear your thoughts. In instances where you worry excessively or want to clear the energy from a disagreement you may have had with someone, ask Jophiel for assistance and allow yourself to relax as she clears your energy.

Archangel Azrael – Death, Dying, Grief

Archangel Azrael is sometimes thought of as the angel of death. It is not something to fear because death is a necessary part of our existence on Earth. Archangel Azrael is always amongst the spiritual teams of mediums, hospice workers, funeral directors, and anyone that assists in the physical death process, whether it is before or after death. He also assists with grief of any kind, whether from the death of a person or relationship of any kind.

I received affirmation that I had Archangel Azrael with me when I went back to Corporate America and got a job working on death settlements in the financial services industry. I already knew I was a medium, but the synchronicity is that I help dead people whether it is in a traditional or non-traditional way. The affirmation of that in my structured job was not a coincidence.

Color: Ecru

You can call on Archangel Azrael if you are grieving a loved one, whether it is a recent loss or not. If you have experienced heartbreak in your life, call on Archangel Azrael to assist you and take some of the grief.

Archangel Ariel – Animals, Environment

Archangel Ariel has the face of a Lion because she is known as the Lioness of God. Ask for her assistance with any issue pertaining to an animal. She can help you find the right animal to adopt or help with things such as behavior issues with animals in your life. She cares for our Earth's environment and is particularly close to anyone that feels called to work on environmental issues.

Color: Light Pink

If you feel connected to faeries and wish to see them or know they are there, ask Archangel Ariel for help in doing so. You will receive the answers in the form of thoughts, feelings, and synchronicities regarding faeries. The fairies are connected to the outdoors and so is Archangel Ariel.

Archangel Nathaniel – Life changes

Archangel Nathaniel has been very present with all the lightworkers experiencing life changes. He has had more presence on Earth recently, with all the vast changes that have been happening in our lives, whether good or bad. Some of these changes come to help us towards our life purpose. Archangel Nathaniel is here to help us with that transition.

I did not know that this was an archangel I had near me until I realized that one of my favorite colors is red. I have a red car, red phone, red jacket, you name it. I have also experienced many life changes, particularly recently.

Color: Red

Call upon Archangel Nathaniel to assist with the ease in transition during your life changes. If you feel that it has been hard, tell him and ask for his assistance. If you want a life change, such as career better suited to your life purpose, ask him.

Archangel Metatron – Akashic Records, Children

Archangel Metatron is one of two archangels who lived as mortals before becoming archangels. On Earth, he was known as the profit Enoch. He has now ascended to the heavens to continue his work as a scribe by recording all of the information in and for the Akashic records. Metatron is also present on the spiritual team of all Indigo children and adults, and he is a helper to anyone that wishes to teach children for the greatest and highest good of all involved.

Color: Turquoise Blue/Green

Ask Archangel Metatron for help if you want to balance your chakras. He can do so with his sacred geometry. He starts balancing your chakras on the top of your head, with a sphere-shaped energy that contains the sacred geometry used to achieve balance.

Archangel Sandalphon – Answered Prayers, Music

Archangel Sandalphon is one of two archangels that lived as mortals before ascending to Heaven as archangels. As a mortal, he was known as the prophet Elijah. His main role is to help carry unanswered prayers to God. He also is associated with music. When I tune into him, I often see him with a sitar or guitar. Those that play a stringed instrument are close to his cause, and all musicians may call upon him for assistance with perfecting their craft or their next musical endeavor.

Color: Rainbow

If you have a prayer that you feel has not been answered, ask Archangel Sandalphon to help deliver your message to God.

Archangel Uriel – God's Light

Archangel Uriel is a very wise archangel that is often associated with shedding light to situations. He helps with Earthly disasters such a flood. He is known for alerting Noah to board the arc before the flood occurred. Uriel has a brilliant yellow-gold energy. Whenever I tune into this archangel, I see him behind what looks like a silver chariot. He has amassed esoteric knowledge and can also help with divine alchemy.

Color: Bright Yellow.

Archangel Uriel has a softer energy than most archangels. When you call upon him, you may feel a light breeze that feels like a soft breeze on a warm summer day. Ask Archangel Uriel to help you see the light in any situation. If you are in a relationship of any sort where you feel your judgment may be clouded or you are not seeing all the truth of the situation, ask Archangel Uriel to help you see the situation clearly.

Archangel Haniel – Grace

Archangel Haniel is a great holder of mystic wisdom. She can be called upon with grace in any situation, particularly something like a job interview or public appearance you may be nervous about. She has a gentle, mysterious energy and is also associated with the moon. Haniel can help you access the information in your soul about crystals and other healing remedies.

Color: Pale Blue

Call upon Archangel Haniel if you are nervous about a performance of any kind where the right words are required. These events include job interviews, not knowing what to say to a friend or lover, or when there has been a communication misunderstanding of some sort.

Archangel Zadkiel – Mercy

Archangel Zadkiel helps with forgiveness. He is also known for assisting people who need to help someone else access information in their memory. He is particularly helpful with accessing the answers you already know during a test.

Color: Midnight Blue

Call upon Archangel Zadkiel if you need help with forgiving yourself or others. It can be a current or past situation. If you have someone that you need to forgive, ask Archangel Zadkiel to help you do so in all directions of time.

Archangel Raziel – Secrets of God

Archangel Raziel is a keeper of the esoteric wisdom of God. He knows all the secrets of the universe, and he is one of the main overseers of the Akashic records. Call upon him to access esoteric information and for help with alchemy and manifestation.

Color: Plum (dark purple)

Call upon Archangel Raziel if you feel guided to work with Akashic records in any way or if you need help remembering a piece of your life purpose. He will guide to you the esoteric secrets in your soul and help you remember and apply divine manifestation principles in your life.

Archangel Raguel – Fairness and Harmony

Archangel Raguel's name means "Friend of God". He oversees all the relationships between archangels and angels. He helps add balance and harmony to relationships, and he is known for helping restore justice for the greatest and highest good of all in something such as a legal proceeding.

Color: Orange

Call upon Archangel Raguel to help in balancing drama in current relationships and also to find new relationships that will be for you greatest and highest good and add harmony to your life.

Archangel Jeremiel – Life Review

Archangel Jeremiel's name means "Mercy of God". He often helps others review their life, whether it is a new soul that has crossed over from Earth or to help us access memories in our past from which we can learn and grow.

Color: Dark Yellow

Call upon Archangel Jeremiel to assist with a current life review to help you with your life purpose.

NOTES

CHAPTER 21

ANGEL HEALINGS

Cord Cutting

In this healing, ask for the assistance of Archangel Michael to come in and cut the cords of fear-based energy from your client in a gentle, loving way. Ask that he also vacuum the energy of your client's body from head to toe of any fear-based energy or energy that does not serve your client's greatest and highest good. Also, you can tell your client how you helped them and that they can ask for the assistance of Archangel Michael to do the same thing for them daily and also to their loved ones (with the soul's permission of the loved ones). Just ask Archangel Michael to do it with the permission of that person's soul if that person does not know that it is happening.

Past Life Healing

Ask Archangel Jeremiel and/or the goddess Isis to help clear the effects of all past life issues your client may have, in all directions of time. For instance, if your client says she is in a relationship where she feels there are issues that are not good and that it may be from a past life, you can do this healing on your client (with their permission).

Another example would be that you have a client that says that she has always been afraid of heights and she does not know why. This may be a past life issue. Many times, the phobias that someone experiences are most likely a past life issue. A person I know has always had a fear of snakes. Not a normal, healthy fear of snakes. The type of fear where he has blocked any TV channel that may possibly show a snake, even in passing. When I asked him where all the animal-related channels were, he told me he programmed them out because "they might have snakes." This is a strong example that there is likelihood that he has a past life issue with them of some sort.

This is NOT a past life regression. You will most likely not ascertain details about the client's past life. If that is what they want and you do not have the proper training, do your best to explain the difference to them and point them in the right direction if they want a regression.

This serves to just heal the past (and potentially future) life issues of your client without knowing what they are specifically.

Beautification of Home or Thoughts

In this healing, ask Archangel Jophiel for assistance. Imagine Jophiel's warm, hot-pink energy purifying the thoughts of your client. You may also ask her for assistance in clearing the energy of a person's home and in creating the interior design of a person's home in a beautiful way that best fits that person's greatest and highest good. Tell your clients to *trust* that the details will come in inspiration and all needs will be met, even if they do not yet know the answers as to how.

Life Purpose

Ask Archangel Jeremiel to assist your clients with finding their life purposes. He can assist them with a life review which can lead to the client's finding their life purpose.

Child Conception and Writing

Ask Archangel Gabriel for assistance with child conception or adoption or to help with current children. Also, ask Gabriel for assistance if your client has writer's block or wishes for the ideas or resources to write a book.

Healing

Ask Archangel Raphael to heal your client, and imagine his Emerald Green healing light healing whatever area of your client's body or life that needs healing. Remember to disclose to your clients, always, that you are not a medical professional and that this healing provided is not meant to replace the healing of traditional medical professionals.

Death/Dying/Mediums

Ask Archangel Azrael for assistance when a client has a loved one that died and is grieving over them. This can also help a client who thinks someone may be dying. Not only does Azrael help departed souls cross over into the light, he also assists families and loved ones that are grieving. Archangel Azrael can also assist with a client that has a personal matter of grief, such as heartbreak unrelated to an actual death that may be seen more as the death of a relationship. If you have a client that is a medium and wants to enhance her ability to see or relay messages from deceased loved ones or discover the best way to find clients and/or deliver clients' messages, ask Archangel Azrael for help with this client. You may also ask on behalf of yourself, if that is the case.

In my life, I have always been a medium. An affirmation of this is my current occupation. In my day job, ironically, I do estate settlements for people all day who have assets to claim when their loved one is deceased. So, basically, I look at death certificates all day long for a living. Coincidence? I do not think so. I have always thought to myself that my primary work on this Earth is serving God and Archangel Azrael with those that have loved ones who have passed.

Other Archangel "Specialties"

Assistance with Finding a Lost Item, Assistance with Finding Your Soulmate – Archangel Chamuel

Time and time again, I have called upon Archangel Chamuel when I am searching for something I cannot find, even something as simple as my keys. I ask him for help and notice where I feel led to go. This feeling is not a push or pull. Just let yourself walk or go to the place that is your next reaction. Nine times out of ten, I have found my lost item immediately.

Help with a Test – Archangel Zadkiel

Archangel Zadkiel is a frequent helper of those who ask for his assistance in taking tests or studying for exams.

Help with Children – Archangel Metatron

Archangel Metatron is especially helpful with Indigo children.

Help with Music – Archangel Sandalphon

If you are a musician or need help with music of any kind,

Archangel Sandalphon can assist.

Help with Animals or Environmental Issues – Archangel Ariel

NOTES

CHAPTER 22

ASCENDED MASTERS

Ascended masters are ethereal beings that help us from the other side. They are teachers that help us with wisdom they gained in their lifetime(s) on Earth. I frequently call upon them to assist me and know that I have a few in my spiritual team. It is quite likely that you do, too.

I am listing information about the ascended masters I feel drawn to; this is not all of them, by any means. My hope is that this helps alert you to the esoteric help you have available to you. If you feel particularly drawn to one or more of them, there is a good chance they have been by your side all along. All you have to do is ask, and they will help you.

Because the ascended masters have lived one or more lifetimes on Earth, they have a more human type of energy in that they have had human emotions and ego as a result. Unlike angels, who are without ego or judgment of any kind, they should be respected emotionally, like you would one of your family or friends.

Goddesses

There are many goddesses from many different times and places: Greece, Egypt, Ireland, Rome, and more. Like angels, you can ask for the help of any goddess. But, unlike angels, they were once human. This means that they have the presence of a human ego, unlike an angel who exudes and only sees love. The goddesses are only good, but I would like to tell you a story about how I experienced the presence of the ego of a goddess.

I like to work with the Celtic goddess Dana, often in my home. One day, she surprised me for some reason, and it frightened me, which I think caused me to yell. I asked her to please respect my boundaries in a very stern tone. Dana went away, and, no matter how I called, she stayed away for over a year. She is back, thank goodness, but that was an example to me to always be respectful to our esoteric helpers—especially those that have been human before because they still have an ego-like aspect to their personalities, just as they did when they were human.

I often call upon what I refer to as the "traffic goddesses" in rush-hour traffic. For me, the traffic goddesses are usually Isis, Brigid, and Dana or Rhiannon. When I call upon them and ask them to clear the traffic, it usually clears quite effectively. I was on the phone with my grandma once, stuck in rush-hour to get to her house for dinner. I told her I would likely be late, but then I called upon the traffic goddesses. As if by magic, one lane of three suddenly cleared, and I got to Gram's house in twenty minutes instead of forty-five to fifty. When I got there, she was surprised. I said, "We can thank the traffic goddesses."

I am listing the goddesses that I most commonly work with or feel guided to share in this book, but there are many others.

Isis (Ancient Egypt)

Isis was married to Osiris and is known for having brought him back from the dead with magic. They then went on to have their son, Horus. She can help with past life issues and magic of any kind. Call on her for a cape of protection when you go into crowds or are in harsh energy.

Dana (Celtic)

Dana is an ancient Celtic goddess whom the Tuatha De´ Danaans followed as their creator. The Tuatha De´ Danaans later transformed into leprechauns when Ireland was invaded by Gaelics. She can help you with manifestation, alchemy, and divine magic. She also can help you with the elemental kingdom, especially leprechauns.

Brigid (Celtic)

She is a Celtic triple goddess, which means that she represents young daughter, mother, and grandmother. She has fiery, warrior-like energy and, in many ways, is the female counterpart to the warrior energy represented by Archangel Michael. Call on her for protection or help in anything, and she will come to your aide.

Hathor (Egyptian)

Hathor is an Egyptian goddess that has the head of the cow. She represents nurturing and mothering. Call on her to assist with mothering and child bearing/adopting.

Kuan Yin (East/Asia)

Kuan Yin is the goddess of love and compassion and is, in

many ways, the Mother Mary of the East. She is committed to staying near Earth to help those that wish to call upon her with compassion and peace. She is a protector of women and children and can help awaken psychic awareness, as well.

Athena (Greek)

Athena is the daughter of Zeus, and she champions all that ask her for protection and assistance. She is tireless in her quest to help those that ask and is known for using wit rather than weapons to resolve battles.

Aphrodite (Greek)

Aphrodite is the Greek goddess of love and passion. She is associated with the planet Venus. She oversees the beautification of all things: love, relationships, homes, and thoughts. She loves 'love' and shows me the balance of the scales in relation to her work with harmony and relationships.

Maeve (Celtic)

Maeve is a Celtic goddess that balances the feminine aspects of cycles. Call upon her for help with menstrual issues such as cramps or the balance of a cycle. She also helps with menopause and birthing, labor, and delivery.

Guinevere (Celtic)

Guinevere connects back to the Arthurian era of Avalon. She was married to King Arthur, but it is said she truly loved Lancelot. Call upon her for matters concerning true love, for it is her utmost passion to assist with that aspect of human life.

Rhiannon (Welsh)

Rhiannon is a goddess and sorceress associated with the moon. She has long, reddish/brown hair down to the small of her back. She rides a white horse. She assists with the crossing over of spirits to the afterworld. Call upon her for help with divine magic, animals, and spirit communication.

Diana (Roman)

Diana is a Roman goddess who always has a bow and arrow. Her mother bore her and her twin brother painlessly, so she is associated with painless childbirth. Call upon her for that, as well as for assistance with nature and animals.

Vesta (Roman)

Vesta is the Roman goddess of home and hearth. Call upon her for help with making changes to a home, acquiring a new home, and filling your home or other surroundings with loving energy and beautiful things.

Abundantia (Roman)

Abundantia is a Roman and Norse goddess associated with fortune and prosperity. She is known for always carrying a bag of gold coins, and you can often recognize her presence when you find coins at random around you. Call upon her for abundance of any kind and know that she is eager to help those who call.

Sarasvati (Hindu)

Sarasvati is the Hindu goddess of the arts. She helps with

all forms of creation involving the arts, including public speaking of any kind. When I see Sarasvati, she shows me a picture of her with a musical instrument and says that she loves art of all kinds. She especially enjoys helping those that wish to express song in any way.

Lakshmi (Hindu)

Lakshmi is a Hindu goddess represented in pictures with many hands and a lotus flower. She works closely with Ganesh (ascended master), and she will help with abundance of any kind. Lakshmi can help you open your arms to receive the abundance in which you seek, and she is a sign of good fortune.

Mawu (Africa)

Mawu is a West African moon goddess who is near to make sure that Mother Earth is not harmed and that we receive the abundance needed to help with environmental issues of any kind.

Pele (Hawaii)

Pele is the Hawaiian goddess of volcanoes who is associated with fire and passion. Call upon Pele to help you feel and find your true passion. She also wishes to be called upon by anyone that wants help in visiting or moving to Hawaii.

Other Ascended Masters

King Solomon

King Solomon ruled Israel from 970-931 BC. He is an

ascended master that is often sought by many, but he doesn't speak to all. It is a privilege to have King Solomon answer you. When I have asked him for assistance, I have been guided to approach him as I would approach a king in a temple or holy place. He is sometimes associated with a flash of blue light. If you see a blue sparkle or flash and think of him, then rest assured it is his presence.

Ganesh

Lord Ganesh is a Hindu deity with the face of an elephant. Just as an elephant would be able to clear pathways more effortlessly than others, so can Ganesh help you overcome your obstacles. Just call his name and ask him to help you with anything you have felt blocked about lately, including something such as writers block. He helps you see truth in your perceived obstacle and can ultimately help you overcome them if you ask. Conversely, he may also block your path, as would a large elephant if you were following behind it. If this occurs when you ask for the help of Ganesh, it is for your greatest and highest good.

Merlin

Merlin is an ancient sorcerer associated with Avalon. While there has been debate over whether he was real or not, he is truly an ascended master that holds esoteric wisdom of the ages. He knows your needs before you do and only usually works with lightworkers. He is here to help and teach others.

Mother Mary

Mother Mary is the Mother of Jesus. She encourages us with the understanding that we do not have to be Roman Catholic or a Christian to believe that she will come to all those that call on her. Her love is non-denominational, and she wishes to wrap her arms around all that need her most. She is particularly close to children's issues of any kind, including the self-care of your own inner child. Her love is gentle and nurturing, and she is associated with the color light blue that so many associate with her in pictures.

Saint Germain

Saint Germain is a French count that was known for many magical abilities and esoteric tools. He has a charismatic yet mysterious energy. He was a royal in his time and was associated with having discovered the fountain of youth, as he was a master at alchemy. Call upon him for any esoteric knowledge you wish to recall. He loves to help those that wish to reconnect with their soul and help others, and he usually comes to you before you even know you need him. He helps with matters of justice, as well as helping to effect change on a global level for the better. Saint Germain will appear for spiritual students and teachers, especially those that teach alchemy and other esoteric wisdom. He works closely with Archangel Michael and, in such, has a purple energy associated with him.

Thoth

Thoth is the Egyptian god of writing and esoteric arts, among many things. He is associated with Atlantis and Free Masonry and has lived many lifetimes beyond that. He says he will likely live on earth as a human, again. He has the no nonsense energy associated with the Indigo and specializes in truth, even truth that is locked behind barriers of space or time. Call upon him for guidance in any kind of writing assistance or understanding. He will also help recall the capacity for alchemy that lies within your soul. Thoth says if you call upon him, you likely have lived a life with him before in Atlantis, Egypt, or both.

NOTES

CHAPTER 23

PAST LIVES

I have a feeling you likely have heard this term before. Perhaps you have an opinion on it, or perhaps not. Most of us have very old souls and have lived many lives before this one. Do you have an affinity towards any particular past era or time? Some of us may associate with the Civil War, some with Atlantis, and some may even feel drawn to biblical times. They can be what you think of as real, or they can even be to places you have imagined such as Avalon and the story of Excalibur. Perhaps some of the things that you are fascinated with involve outer space. Have you had a lifelong obsession with UFOs? If there is any time period or place that you feel consistently drawn to? If a time period or place shapes your life in any way, the odds are very good that you have lived a past life there.

I have a tattoo that says "Lady Day" as a tribute to Billie Holiday. I name all of my pets after musicians from that same jazz era (of the 1930s-1950s). I have had cats named after Dinah Washington, Charlie Parker, and Nina Simone. Do you think I may have had a past life related to that? I also have many Paris-themed items in my home. I took a trip to Paris (and loved it) which later led to my pursuit of learning the French language. This also points to the fact that I have lived a past life in or near Paris, France. When I recently told someone I knew that I loved the poppy flower, she pointed out that that was a symbol of World War I in France, and the hair stood up on the back of my neck. A friend of mine wanted to visit every American Civil War battleground. That's likely not coincidence. So, your fascination with another time or place may extend to the point where you decorate your house like that time and place, dress in that era, or consistently visit a foreign place.

There are ways that you can have past life regressions or healings, and you can even do a guided meditation recording if you feel led to. You could even get a reading about it or ask your guides and angels for a dream about a past life that you can easily remember when you wake up. If you have a fear of something and you just cannot figure out where the fear came from, it is likely from another lifetime. Fears such as these can include claustrophobia or having a dramatic fear of snakes. There are practitioners that can help you with hypnosis and regression to explore these past lives in order to heal your current life. My friend has an over-the-top fear of snakes, to the point where he programmed all channels out of his TV that might even air a glimpse of a snake. I do not particularly like snakes, but he simply cannot handle it at all. I often wonder what happened to him in another lifetime with snakes.

There are common past life memories in many lightworkers. We often think we have a block in regards to our gifts. We have a fear of telling anyone that we might be psychic or mediums. This stems from having one or several lifetimes in which we have been persecuted for our esoteric gifts. Many of us have memories and fears associated with the Salem witch trials. We came to life and were burned at the stake—sometimes repeatedly. I did.

When I asked the question to my spiritual team as to the reason, I was just told it was to bring awareness and light to the time. If you read that passage and had emotion or a knowing come up, it is likely that you were also alive at that time and persecuted as a witch.

Many of us also have a history of drowning in Atlantis. Yes, Atlantis. I remember as a little girl, whenever someone would mention Atlantis, the hair would stand up on the back of my neck, and it fascinated me. The first time I nearly drowned, in this life, was around the age of three or four. So, most of us that have a history associated with Atlantis have or had an unnatural fear of drowning. I did not think I did, and then my mother reminded me that I had a terrible fear of the pool or drowning as a small child. If you are from Atlantis, you resonate with this information. You likely have many rocks or crystals that you either have in your home as a decoration or even use for healing. You probably respect the fact that they need to be cleared in the moon and absorb energy or even feel alive. You like to be always near the water and probably know how to swim quite well, but you do not need to be in the water and probably have an aversion to the thought of sailing on a ship. Once I figured out I was from Atlantis, I realized people that are usually close to me, even being more than an acquaintance, were there in some way.

I did not know what to make of these places that I had always thought were fictitious but discovered were real. Then, however, I asked my guides what life the people at a job I had were from, and they simply said, "Avalon."

All of the sudden, I could feel that energy and knew it was true. Even more interesting is the fact that my middle name is Jennifer. Jennifer is a modern day version of the name Guinevere, like the Guinevere from Avalon who is an ascended master (goddess) today. So, if your name is

Jennifer, you likely have a connection to Guinevere, too. It does not necessarily mean we were her, but it is a validation that we likely were there in Avalon at the time of Guinevere, Lancelot, and King Arthur.

If you read this information and thought, "I don't believe that," that is okay. I am not sure I even believed it when I first heard it. But the more that I do this, the more my mind opens to new ideas. What I do believe, without a doubt, is that past lives are real. Our soul is eternal, and many of us have been spiritual teachers in many lifetimes and volunteered to come to do that and help others again.

NOTES

CHAPTER 24

AKASHIC RECORDS

The Akashic records are something known to contain the collective consciousness of ALL. All happenings on Earth and within the planetary system are often thought of as a library. This is how I think of them.

The first visit I consciously made to the Akashic records was when I went to a meditation for Akashic records that was part of a group meditation. I went thinking it was a class, and then realized it was a meditation to see our own Akashic library. The facilitator told us that you can only access the Akashic records with *permission* from whoever guards them. (I clairaudiently hear as I type this that it is a committee called *The Elders* who are stewards of God). The facilitator then told us that we should have an intention of what we want to know before we did our journey (meditation) to visit our records. With that, I set the intention of wondering my purpose for moving to Boston, where I lived at the time, having just moved 1,400 miles to be there.

As we started the journey, at first I could not see anything.

I thought, "Oh, great. I came all the way here and do not even have permission to go in to see my Akashic records."

Then, all of the sudden, the staircase to the Hall of Records, as they are sometimes also referred to as, appeared. At first, when I entered, it looked to me like a huge library that I imagined in a grand castle, with books from wall to wall and ceiling to floor. I feel as if it may have been a record of universal events because I had to pass through them to get to my own personal Akashic records. Mine were in an entirely different place.

Let me preface the moment of entering the room of my records by telling you that, until that point, I had always had this idea that I was going to *graduate* after this lifetime and never have to live on Earth as a human again.

As I entered the room where my soul's records live, my intent was to see the *volume* or *volumes* that represented the purpose for my moving to Boston. As if by magic, that volume's spine came up and showed itself to me; and it was the surname of a good male friend of mine. We had once been romantically involved years before, long distance, before I moved to Boston. Well, there I was living in Boston, and he lived in Boston and was still one of my best friends. I heard that this was the main driver of my coming, to see if we could create the marriage and family we had never been able to create in all our other lifetimes of unrequited love together on Earth. It made sense, even though I was initially disappointed it was not something a bit more universally profound.

Well, this person still remains one of my best friends on Earth. It is as if we have known each other forever, and apparently we have! We have collectively chosen not to create that family in this lifetime. But I feel that we made some progress in this lifetime because we were able to have romance and then later decided that was not right for us and that we were better as friends. Now that we did not accomplish the goal of marriage and family, I figure we will see each other in future lifetimes until we do.

When I saw the spine of that volume of my Akashic records that I just detailed, it was as if all the volumes of my souls' journey were in a vertical line in front and in back of me, kind of like a super highway. When I saw how many volumes were in front of that volume, I groaned, knowing it meant this was not likely my *graduation* lifetime as I had hoped. I have since had that affirmed because I have had a visit from my future self. Just for a moment, but I knew it was me from a future time.

I believe that before we come to Earth for each human lifetime, we sit at tables with our soul families or people we are going to do work with in this lifetime and all write contracts based on what our life lessons and plans are to be. So, I have seen myself sit at many tables with my various family members such as my father's side of the family and others. I have even heard others speak of their experiences. Someone once told me that she had a regression and communication with her abusive father. This gave them the opportunity for healing in the form of the father apologizing and taking accountability for his actions. He then explained that they all had a contract of the lessons they were going to learn in this life. As their family all sat at the heavenly table to make their contracts to come into this life, it was as if they were seeing a script and casting the characters to be whom they would become in this life. When it came time to agree on who was to be the abusive father, it was the most loving and giving of them all that agreed that he would take on the role, for no one else wanted it.

I have seen a few of the various tables I was at with others in my soul family with whom I was contracting to be with in this life. I do not even quite understand what all the contracts are or mean yet, but that is a part of the journey on Earth. I have even seen one of my spiritual teachers at one of my tables as a member of my soul family. I do not know what the details were, but it validated that we were likely contracting that she would be my teacher at some point in this life.

I had a dream of three people I know sitting at a dining room table with me. In my mind, it was an unlikely group to be dining together. After the dream, when I was reviewing it mentally, I realized it was probably symbolizing the contracts that our souls made before coming to Earth.

The Akashic records are also said to contain the history of all the planets and events on the planets, so it is not limited to just our lives alone. It is, however, very helpful to be able to access this information when trying to ascertain parts of your life.

NOTES

CHAPTER 25

THE TIME IS NOW

This is the end of this book but not the end of your journey. You can read as much as you need to about this. I am a constant student no matter how much I grow in this, and I am sure you will be, too. The world needs you now. Not when you are perfect. Not when you are the master of your craft. You chose to be on this Earth at this time for this purpose: to help others. It is time to get yourself out there, if only a little at a time. Every step in the direction of your dreams is usually the best step.

We have discussed several times in this book that you may not know what your exact purpose is. That may lead you to feelings of impatience or frustration. Part of your impatience is that you are such a powerful manifestation at a soul level that it is hard for you to wait for the physical to catch up. You have had these gifts in many other lifetimes. You are an old soul. If you have not yet found the person to save you or the beacon of light you are looking for, then YOU are that light. You are the person to save and help others.

Think of how many times you have thought to yourself of something such as music, a poem, a book, or a teacher that saved your life in some, or many, ways. It is time for you to give some of the gratitude that you felt in those moments back to the universe. Know that you have all the information that you need in your heart, head, and soul already. Ask the universe to help you do what you need to do, and take guided action. If I had never done so, I would never had written this book or taught the students I have taught or helped the clients that I have helped. It is scary sometimes to put yourself out there, but the worst that can happen is that you can hear a "no" or something to that effect. Think of all the celebrities you know of that have had stories about how many times they heard the word "NO" before they were a success. What if they had stopped?

Know that you are perfect just as you are. Try to stop being so hard on yourself. Know that you are exactly where you are supposed to be right now. Trust that the rest will fall into place when you take guided action in the direction of your dreams. Thank you for being on this planet at this time. You are needed, supported, and loved by the heavens.

Namaste.

BIBLIOGRAPHY

Archangels and Ascended Masters by Doreen Virtue

Ascended Masters Oracle Deck by Doreen Virtue

Goddess Guidance Oracle Deck by Doreen Virtue

Realms of the Earth Angels by Doreen Virtue

You Can Heal Your Life by Louis L. Hay

Ask and It Is Given by Esther and Jerry Hicks

RECOMMENDED READING

You Can Heal Your Life by Louise L. Hay

Ask and It Is Given by Esther by Jerry Hicks

Realms of the Earth Angels by Doreen Virtue

Born Knowing by John Holland

The Angel Therapy Handbook by Doreen Virtue

The Gift by Echo Bodine

The Crystal Bible by Judy Hall

ABOUT THE AUTHOR

Lisa Andres lives near Minneapolis, Minnesota. In addition to being a psychic, medium, and author, she is a voracious reader who loves good stories and never leaves home without her e-reader. Lisa is a graduate of McNally Smith College of Music; she sings and plays piano. She loves writing, pets, live music, and all things New England.

Indigo Warrior

A Guide for Indigo Adults
& the Parents of Indigo Children

By Lisa Andres

INTRODUCTION TO
INDIGO WARRIOR

I am a psychic medium. I am an author. I am a singer. I am also an Indigo.

I had no idea what an Indigo was until a few years ago. Like many others that are around New Age reading material or shops and find themselves with like minds, I had heard the term "Indigo" swirl around me in reference to children and never had explored it.

In a class I had for mediums in 2009, the teacher referred to me as "Indigo Warrior." She said, "Hello, Indigo Warrior." I looked behind me, wondering if she was talking to someone else. She wasn't. I shrugged my shoulders, having no idea what that meant, and said hello back to her. Several times during that weekend class, she addressed me as "Indigo Warrior." I made a mental note to look further into what an Indigo was when I got home.

When I later looked into the term "Indigo," I realized that there were not a lot of books out there about Indigos. Most of them are for Indigo children. That drove me to address Indigo adults as well as children in this book. I'm an Indigo adult, and I wanted to share the information that I have learned in the years since I was first addressed as Indigo Warrior.

I was inspired to write this book when listening to a friend of mine as she told me about her daughter's anger. She didn't understand it. She didn't think that she and her husband had done anything as parents to cause the anger, but, like good parents, they still felt responsible. They were starting to wonder how to deal with it. When they told me about one situation, a light bulb went on in my head showing me that her daughter was an Indigo. So I began to arm her with some information.

In my practice as a psychic medium, I started to draw Indigo adults and children to me in my readings. The best thing about what I do is seeing the relief in people who realize that they are finally being understood, to know that they are Indigos and finally have a confirmation of all the things they have been through.

I later had another class with the teacher that had originally called me Indigo Warrior. In that second class, she asked the people that were Indigos to stand. In a crowd of hundreds of people, a handful of us hesitantly stood. She then asked the rest of the audience to give us a round of applause because the Indigos were the people here to help in leading the way for others.

It is my hope in writing some of my experiences with and about Indigos that it helps you. You are very important to the world right now.

WHAT IS AN INDIGO?

An Indigo is a lightworker who was called to Earth as the result of prayers for positive changes to our planet. A lightworker is someone with a global purpose and an individual life purpose. A global purpose is a life purpose that helps others in some way, in addition to themselves. A lightworker may also be known as an Earth Angel. It is called a global life purpose because helping others could extend to a potentially global level.

There was chaos that erupted on Earth in World War I and II. The first large influx of lightworkers in our current generation came to Earth as a result of the prayers for peace and resolution of the Earth's problems. This is better known as the "Baby Boom" of the 1950s. Many of the people from the Baby Boomer generation were the parents of the large influx of adult Indigos.

Indigos are born to bring truth and justice to the world. Many Indigos have a very warrior-like presence. They are born tough. They are often born to speak truth. They have a natural lie detector and can detect inauthentic character in others. They may have been punished at some point in their lives for not being able to hold their tongues.

They are on what seems to be a constant search for truth and justice. They see through the character of others easily and are not patient with character flaws or with someone they don't trust. For instance, if they sense that someone is not exactly what he or she seems, even if Indigos have no proof of it, they trust the sense that something is off about the person. Most other people would give a person they had a bad feeling about a chance, only to learn the hard way. Indigos trust that inner truth detector and honor it right away. They won't give anyone the time of day that they don't trust or have a bad vibe about for any reason. They commonly come without a filter, so to speak, because they represent truth and have a hard time keeping their truth to themselves.

Indigos often wonder why they were dropped off on this planet because they've never felt like they belong. They spend their whole life feeling different, and they may spend time trying to fit in only to realize it doesn't suit them. Indigos are born to be different.

Indigos generally are, or think they are, the smartest people they know. They may not make the best classroom students because they grow impatient and oftentimes think they are smarter than the teacher. Often they already know the information they are being given. They have a tendency to either be asked to skip ahead grades, or they completely flunk out of school or drop out of school because they are frustrated with the entire process.

Patience is not a virtue that is found in abundance in Indigos. They know they have a big life purpose even if they don't know exactly what it is. They have no patience for dishonesty or corruption of any kind. They are born with a huge sense of purpose. They can get frustrated at a young age when they have an inner knowing they are here on Earth for a special mission, but they may not know what that mission is, or have the capacity to execute it, in their young years.

Many Indigos tend to be born into dysfunction of some sort. That may mean dysfunction in the family home or stressful situations in childhood. Many Indigos were, or are, bullied in school.

Indigos may become lawyers to fight laws that no longer

serve us. They are soldiers, police officers, or work in some capacity to protect others.

Indigos do not feel like they can fit in a box. Ever. No matter the category, they have never completely fit. That frustrates them, but that is also one of the many things that helps push them towards their life purpose. They break the box and make new categories that fit; in doing so, they lead the way for others.

Indigos have a strong sense of independence. They are natural leaders and want to do things their own way. They have an intense presence, and they will take the command of a room just upon entering it. Some Indigos may be tossed into leadership positions, whether they like it or not. Many Indigos have a tendency to get fired from or lose jobs. Because of this, they are often self–employed and are their own bosses. As a result, many Indigos are entrepreneurs.

Indigos tend to be a handful as children, as they have no shortage of energy. Overall, more than anything, Indigos feel misunderstood. That starts when they are children. They tend to have a lot of energy and don't know what to do with it. They may be put on a medication at some point because those around them can't deal with such intense, restless energy. Indigos might be diagnosed with Attention Deficit Disorder (ADD), Attention Deficit Hyperactivity Disorder (ADHD), or Post Traumatic Stress Disorder (PTSD).

Many Indigos have a serious look on their faces. They have what some describe as an "old soul" that has experienced its share of pain. Many are asked, "Why do you always look so serious?" One of the reasons for that serious or penetrating look in their eyes is that they are old souls who have seen the destruction and sadness that can happen on Earth many times. They may not come across that way, but the depth in the experience of their soul, whether in this lifetime or others, knows that life is serious and heavy. It's one of the things Indigos are here to help others with: the heaviness of Earth when things need to change. They inherently know they are here for an important mission.

The injustices of Earth upset these lightworkers. Indigos may be pet rescuers, people rescuers, law changers, charity founders, and more. They are the whistle blowers. They want justice and won't stop until they get it.

Indigos have a tendency to be tattooed, pierced, emo, Goth, or anything else that expresses their discontent and need to be understood. They are quite familiar with curse words and use them regularly. It's not that they don't know how to speak properly; it's just that they have to honor their truth at any price. Making people uncomfortable is something Indigos seem to be good at, so at some point they just learn to go with the flow of that and express themselves in whatever way they see fit.

The bottom line is this: Indigos are here to help people, young or old. Indigos have no set age. Many adult Indigos were born in the 1970s, but you can be older than that and still be an Indigo. My grandmother believes that she is an Indigo. There is a large influx of Indigo children that have been born in the last forty years, and it is not going to stop any time soon. I am one of those Indigos, so I can personally relate to many of these characteristics.

Like so many Indigos, I was bullied in school for much of my childhood. I was often punished as a child for not being able to hold my tongue. As an adult, I was thrust into a leadership role. In my career in corporate America, I found out my boss was leaving one day, and I took over managing the team for him the next.

We, as Indigos, are here to pave the way for others, to lead by example, to show others the way. Even if we have no idea how to do that, or that we are even doing it, we often set an example just in our very being. We stand for truth, and whether we present as a bad boy, a smart girl, or whatever it may be, our very presence demands attention. People can't help but notice, and we set an example because of it. Others need our help or for us to show them the way by doing whatever it is that we are good at. We are truth. We are leaders. We are honest. We are angry. We want justice. We will stop at no cost to do what's right.

This world needs Indigos. It needs you or your child that is an Indigo. You have not lived your life for nothing. You have not been abused or felt like you didn't fit in for nothing. You were incarnated for this time to help others. You are not alone, even if you have felt like it your whole life.

You are a warrior.

You are beautiful.

You are an Indigo.

HOW DO I KNOW IF I AM AN INDIGO?

Traits of the Indigo:

- Wise, expressive eyes
- Warrior-like presence
- Truth-speaking
- Justice-seeking
- Intelligent
- Angry
- Powerful
- Sharp tongue
- Impatience
- Prone to addiction
- Often diagnosed as ADD, ADHD, PTSD

Have you always felt you've been misunderstood? Like maybe you were dropped off on the wrong planet or were just in the wrong family? Do you feel like you have had to constantly apologize for who you are? Or that your energy is too intense for others to be around? Have you had times when you just wished you were more normal? Have you ever been referred to as "a bull in a china shop" or something similar?

You have always felt like the different one, and, in many instances, the family you grew up in made it abundantly clear that you were different from them, which lead to feeling isolated even more.

You've always been a leader, whether you wanted to be or not. You are somehow always nominated to be the boss, or you just plain enjoy being the boss. You certainly could not handle anyone being your boss. You might have been fired a time or two because you could not take being told what to do for one minute longer. Now, you are your own boss, and that suits you well. If you haven't been a formal leader, you've been a leader in some way, even if it was just paving the way for others by taking the first step on an unknown road.

You have often been told that you look too serious, or too mean, or that you should "smile more." You might be tattooed and pierced because it's the best way you can express yourself. Maybe you have even dyed your hair pink just to stand out. You were aware long ago that you always stand out whether you like it or not, so you do it on your own terms.

You had a hard time in school; you might have had a learning disability or just a general impatience for the school and teachers. Sometimes you felt smarter than the teacher; that may have led to you either leaving school or transitioning to a different school that better fit your needs.

You're not a stranger to a fight, but you are not always looking for one. You fight, or have fought, to protect yourself or people around you. It might even be your job to protect others in some way.

You have a hard time keeping your opinion to yourself. You have been told that you need a filter on your mouth or need to learn how to shut your mouth. You can sense the character of another person at first sight and have little patience for small talk. The injustices of the world make you mad.

You like your cigarettes, alcohol, caffeine, or other vices. If this is not a current habit, it could have been one in the past that you have overcome.

You have a past that you don't like to tell people about because you don't want them to pity you. Your childhood was dysfunctional and abusive: physically, verbally, or both. You may have been sexually abused or raped at some point. You may have been told you were imagining the abuse when you tried to tell an adult. You may have been in abusive relationships as an adult. Injustice in this world makes you MAD. You cannot stand to see someone abused or treated unfairly.

You've always felt frustrated. You have no idea why. Frustration bubbles inside you at knowing you have a higher purpose but now knowing what that purpose is.

You could not blend in if you tried. You have wished to be normal but never felt normal. You have wished to not be noticed as easily as you are. You have been told your energy is harsh or powerful as if you are doing something wrong in just being. You have felt rejected in many ways, like a misfit of sorts. You have never truly felt that you fit in.

You may have a history of relationship problems. You may be divorced—maybe more than once. You may have moved or changed residences more than is comfortable for you. You may have moved from state to state, or country to country, because you felt called somewhere, only to find yourself right back where you started, and you don't understand why.

You sometimes wonder if you were sent to Earth to be alone. You'd rather be alone than be in a relationship that makes you wish you were alone.

Some days the world feels too heavy. You easily feel like you absorb the heavy energy of crowds. You wonder what on Earth you did to deserve to be here because you know somehow that your soul wouldn't have—couldn't have—chosen this. At the very least, you know you had to be asked to come down to Earth to help others because you couldn't have done it willingly.

If you nodded your head in agreement, and perhaps shed a tear, when reading some or all of these statements, you are indeed an Indigo.

I'm so relieved to have found you and that you have found me.

You are not alone.

CHARACTER TRAITS OF INDIGOS

Vocal

Indigos are born without filters on their mouths. I can't tell you how many times I've heard someone say to me that he or she doesn't have a filter. Whenever I hear that now, I know that the person I'm being told about is probably also an Indigo. I recently met someone who informed me that she did not have a filter. I laughed, knowing that person was probably an Indigo.

As Indigos, we are also born to know truth. When we sense that things are not truthful, we point them out. We have opinions, can't stand to see injustices, and are the first to call someone out on something that we perceive as unjust. Not all Indigos are extremely vocal. Some may be quiet or observers. But when they have something to say, watch out. They don't talk unless they have to, and then they don't quiet down easily.

By saying Indigos' words are often unfiltered, I mean that we don't typically think about what we are going to say before we say it. We spill out our opinions or truths, regardless of how these might hurt or offend the person we are talking to.

I didn't have a filter until I had a job that forced one on me. When I became a manger in corporate America, I learned quickly that I would have to learn how to "talk the talk" and "walk the walk." I used to wonder why there wasn't an unofficial handbook for managers that included in it the language managers should use to be effective. It was hard at first, but gradually it instilled a filter in me both in and outside of work. At least the filter works most of the time.

Indigos are direct. We don't mince words. We don't mean to offend anyone with our sharp tongue. It's just that Indigos believe in truth, and anything else is unimportant. Older indigos may have had many experiences being scolded, slapped across the face, or having their mouths washed out with soap as kids because they just could not seem to control their words even if they knew they'd be punished. Most Indigos don't think about what we are going to say long enough to consider the consequences. We talk first and think about what we said later, and that's only if we have to.

Impatient

Patience is not usually a normal virtue of an Indigo. We were born impatient. It was like we know we have a purpose that is bigger than us and can't wait for it to begin or to figure out what that purpose is.

We have a tendency to lose our tempers rather quickly when our patience is being tested, and, as children, that can bring out the worst in us. As children, we seriously test our parents, and impatience often escalates to tantrums and episodes that our parents don't know what to do with.

As adults, everything Indigos have to do has to be done yesterday. We are all about action steps. When there's not an action step to take, we become impatient. We may form nervous habits like cracking our knuckles to signal our impatience.

One thing that most of us are impatient with is small talk. We simply don't have time for preamble and niceties when it's the heart of the matter, the truth of things, we are trying to get to. We don't want to waste time with fluff when we feel that what we are saying or doing should have a point. We are skeptical of someone who tries to talk too much about the weather or something else when we have no interest in it.

Excellent Judges of Character

Indigos always know whether we will like someone just by sensing their energy. We tend to make good police officers or tend to be in similar professions where we have to make intuitive decisions about the character of another person. We may walk into a place and say we don't like the way it feels and insist upon leaving immediately. We are like this with people, too. We may have a sense of uneasiness or know that a person is not who we want to be around. If it's your child that is the Indigo, they might try to tell you about this feeling concerning another person. You may shush or punish your child for saying this, only to later discover that your child was right when the person they were trying to tell you about hurts you.

Intense

Indigos have a fierce look of intensity in our eyes. Even when we mean to smile, it might look to someone else like we are mad at them. We have a penetrating look in our eyes as if we can see into the souls of others. And sometimes we can. We walk into a room and couldn't blend in if we tried. The ferocity of our energy just seems to precede us as we enter a room. People either look at us like they're trying to figure us out, or they look down because we intimidate them.

Indigos are often asked, "Would you calm your energy down?" I was even asked that once by another psychic medium. It was almost as if the person reading me was frustrated at my powerful energy field. This person then proceeded to tell me that I had to work on toning my energy down so I wouldn't have as harsh of an impact when I enter a room. Sometimes our energy is so big we notice light bulbs mysteriously go off or break when we are near. I have had this happen too many times to be a coincidence.

Indigos know we couldn't be normal if we tried, so most of us stopped trying long ago. I remember once being scolded by one of my bosses for my harsh demeanor. I told him I would try the best I could but that it might be difficult for me to be someone that I'm not. I've grown tired of apologizing to other people for who I am because my very energy, or attitude, offends them.

Sensitive

Indigos are beautifully sensitive people. At times, it can feel like we absorb the sadness of Earth. When we hurt, it impacts us on a very deep level. We may become guarded as a result of that. Underneath the invisible walls that we tend to build around ourselves is a depth of vulnerability that makes us very sensitive. As a result of that, sometimes we get defensive. Our tempers spark easily. What lies beneath that is a sensitivity that is so pure that sometimes we don't know what to do with it. That, in turn, can make our emotions feel heavy.

PORTRAIT OF AN INDIGO:
THE INDIGO CHILD

When I do readings for parents of Indigo children, they come into the reading not knowing the answer they are looking for or the term that fits their child. They just know that they have a child that is different and want to know more about it.

As parents, I can only imagine that you feel that all of your children are special in many wonderful ways. Indigo children are usually the ones that challenge you the most. They are usually the children that you can't control or seem to get to behave no matter what you do.

They may have sudden bouts of anger and become frustrated easily. They usually get bored, seem impatient, and don't seem to know how to quell those feelings. As such, the anger they have can manifest into behaviors that are disruptive, not only to your child but to the rest of your family. They may have been diagnosed, or possibly even misdiagnosed, as having ADD or ADHD. If it's not a typical diagnosis, they still may be on some form of medication to subdue their extra energy or anger.

Indigo children tend to have an endless supply of energy. It can be a good thing, but it can be a highly frustrating thing for a parent when the child never settles down. They are born with a knowing that they have a higher purpose, and I believe that knowing is within their soul and manifests as endless energy. This can also manifest into anger. I write about the anger inherent in the Indigo, and that starts when they are very young.

My best friend's daughter always had endless energy. I know that my friend and her husband were great parents. There were no other children in their home to upset their child, but, as parents, they didn't understand why she always seemed so angry.

One night my friend told me that her then-10-year-old daughter had publicly called another child "stupid," and they had punished her as a result. At that moment, the Indigo within me regressed to my own similar childhood moments. Moments where, as a child, I felt unjustly punished. It may not have been appropriate for the girl to call another child "stupid," but an Indigo speaks his or her truth. That was probably her truth at the moment she said it. She just could have said it a bit better. In hearing that, I felt like that had been the story of my life as I was growing up.

Indigos tend to not have a filter on their mouths, and I don't have to tell you that most children don't have filters. With an Indigo, that is escalated. Indigos are born to speak truth and know the truth before most other people. They will tell you about someone's character, and they are probably right whether you realize that or not.

Some Indigo children may have a hard time in school. They might even get kicked out of school. That is not because they are dumb by any stretch of the imagination. They are just frustrated with the entire learning process. They either feel they are smarter than the teacher or just plain don't have time for school. Some Indigos are prone to learning disabilities which may inhibit their learning in a traditional school environment.

If you have an Indigo child in your home, it may be the one that you are punishing frequently for acting up in some way. You may feel that this child threatens other children in your home in some way. That is not always the case, but it is definitely possible with an Indigo in the home. If you are the parent of an Indigo, you are probably frustrated. You might even feel at your wit's end with your child. You have tried everything and don't know what else to do.

It is also possible that you have a child that meets one or more of these qualities I described but not all of them. Perhaps your child has a more gentle energy most of the time but is prone to sudden outbursts of anger that escalate beyond what you would consider normal.

If you identify with this, it is possible that you have an Indigo child. I must admit that I am not a parent, but in my research and speaking to other parents of Indigo children, I've come up with some suggestions that may help.

Diet

The diet of any child is very important. Indigo children are more susceptible to hyperactivity as a result of the foods that they eat. As a parent, try to be conscious of not letting them have too much sugar, caffeine, or any other stimulant that can take the excess energy of an Indigo and escalate it. Indigo children would also benefit from having as much natural, fresh food in their diet as possible. They are very sensitive to the chemicals and additives found in processed foods.

Anger Outlets

A great outlet for the anger of an Indigo child is physical activity. This may be a traditional sport like basketball or soccer, or it could be something like going to a karate class. It can also be through an activity such as playing a musical instrument or singing. When I was a child, I liked to sing. I would play my records and sing to the top of my lungs. I had no idea it was an outlet for my natural Indigo anger, but it was.

I watched an interview on Oprah's Master Class with Alicia Keys about growing up in a rough neighborhood. Her mother scheduled her after-school activities to keep her so busy that she didn't have time to get into trouble. While I am not saying that Alicia Keys is an Indigo or not, this would be a good practice for any parent wanting to keep their child focused, such as the parent of an Indigo.

Empowerment

Find a way to empower your Indigo child. Indigos are natural born leaders. Find a way to give your child a voice. Indigos are children that need to feel that they have a voice. They need to feel heard. They need to make a difference.

Indigos are also lightworkers. Lightworkers are on Earth to help other people in addition to themselves. Is there a way that you can involve your child with a volunteer project of some sort? You might take them to an animal shelter to give the pets there some attention while the pets wait for their forever home, send a letter to a soldier, or help raise money for other students in need. There are many possibilities based on what the child would like to do and what works for your family.

Create an Environment of Understanding

Overall, more than anything, Indigos feel misunderstood. That starts when Indigos are children. They tend to have a lot of energy and don't know what to do with it. As a result, Indigo children may be diagnosed with ADD or

ADHD. They may be put on a medication because those around them can't deal with their heavy, restless energy. Indigo children have a bright light energetically; the drugs dim that light for a time.

These children are independent thinkers that experience extreme highs and extreme lows. They are precocious and often have a very high intelligence level. They may experience some of their hyperactivity in the classroom as a result of being bored with the course work. These are children that have the capacity to learn, even though they may experience a learning disability. That and other challenges that may arise in the classroom will frustrate this child, and they may start to disrupt the classroom as a result.

Together, you and your family may have to work to find creative, firm solutions for your Indigo child. They are little lightworkers that know they are here to do something special, and that starts in childhood.

BAD DREAMS, FEARS, AND
THE INDIGO CHILD

Every child has fears and bad dreams. Indigo children are sometimes plagued by them. This goes back to the idea that Indigos are very empathic, meaning that they tend to not only feel their own emotions, but the emotions of others. This expands their fears.

Fear is linked closely with anxiety. I interpret that to mean that somehow our bodies are in dissonance with our souls. Our soul might know our true purpose, and that can scare the human part of us. To me, the souls with the biggest purpose are sometimes the ones with the biggest fears. Regardless, it is normal for an Indigo Child to have disrupted sleep patterns and feel terrified when they are young.

When I was a child, I used to have terrible nightmares. I felt like there were eyes staring at me all the time. I felt like there was some unseen force (a bad force) that was in the room with me. Sometimes I would have dreams that I was lost, and I couldn't wake up; I would feel like I wanted to wake up but somehow could not make myself do it. That scared the living daylights out of me. Whether it was a monster I was dreaming about, the devil (my Roman Catholic upbringing insured that I knew all about hell), or some other creature of my mind, I would always run to my parents' room crying in the middle of the night. That I was a little medium and just didn't know it only added to the anxiety. I always sensed spirits around. I know now that I wasn't imagining it, but it scared the daylights out of me at the time. I told my family the things I saw; paired with that and the continual bad dreams, I was sent to a psychiatrist as a young girl. The psychiatrist tried to tell me that the boogie man wasn't real. But it wasn't the boogie man that was haunting me in my dreams. I used to stand on my bed in the middle of the night as if somehow that would protect me from all the spirits I thought were after me.

Your Indigo child may experience something similar. The Indigos that are coming to Earth now are more evolved souls who also may be telling you that they see or talk to dead people, angels, or other supernatural beings. It's important to a little Indigo to feel listened to. Whether or not you believe your child, whether or not you have had enough of what you consider to be your child's nonsense, try your best to let your scared, little Indigo have a voice. He or she came here with a huge life purpose, and your child is likely afraid of all that pressure on his or her soul. Perhaps your child is afraid of all the things that his or her soul knows that your child hasn't yet realized.

I believe that, before we come to Earth, we work with God to plan our lives. Then we are sent to Earth. Our souls may be wise and evolved, but when we come to Earth as babies, our memories of those past lives are taken from us. It's our job on Earth to remember what our soul truly knows, but the process of doing so tends to cause us anxiety and heightens our fears.

If you have a child with night terrors, nightmares, or heightened sensitivity that you don't know what to do with, ask your angels for help. We all have angels that are with us that want to help. The trick is to ask. They can't intervene unless we ask them. Archangel Metatron is the archangel that works with Indigo children. You don't have to remember that name; just pray for help, and, if you think of it, ask the angels for help. Their help comes to you in the form of ideas and thoughts and may come in ways that you don't expect.

You can also try to talk to your child's *oversoul*—that's another term for the higher self. Tell your child that he or she is safe. Sometimes the reason why a child screams the minute it comes from its mother's womb is because to be in a human body is to be away from the energy that is God. The overwhelming peace and unconditional love that we feel when we are with Him in Heaven is suddenly taken from the child. Then we come to Earth and are attached to a body once again, and that feeling disappears. That scares us even as adults and may be a part of why your child is so distressed.

LISA ANDRES

41765934R00108

Made in the USA
Lexington, KY
27 May 2015